W9-BYL-695

# distant partner

## DR. LES CARTER

A
JANET
THOMA
BOOK

THOMAS NELSON PUBLISHERS
Nashville • Atlanta • London • Vancouver

Published in Nashville, Tennessee, by Thomas Nelson, Inc., Publishers, and distributed in Canada by Word Communications, Ltd., Richmond, British Columbia.

**Library of Congress Cataloging-in-Publication Data**

Carter, Les.
   Distant partner : how to tear down emotional walls and communicate with your husband / Les Carter.
      p.    cm.
   ISBN 0-7852-7551-7
      1. Communication in marriage. 2. Communication—Sex differences.
3. Husbands—Psychology. 4. Wives—Psychology. 5. Marriage—Religious
aspects—Christianity. I. Title.
HQ734.C3313   1997
646.7'8—dc21                                                          96-47773
                                                                          CIP

Printed in the United States of America.

2 3 4 5 6 QPK 02 01 00 99 98 97

# contents

## *acknowledgments*

A tremendous thanks to Irene Swindell
for her help in preparing the manuscript
and to Janet Thoma
and the editors of Thomas Nelson.

# ✒ preface

*A*re you a wife whose husband won't make the effort to know and understand you? Do you ever find yourself asking, "Why does he tune out when I try to express my deepest emotions?" Do you feel he is so steeped in his maleness that he can't relate to your communication style or accept your ways as normal or reasonable?

If any of these questions hit home, you've picked up the right book and you are not alone. You probably struggle more than you would like to admit with insecurity, anger, disillusionment, and miscommunication. Perhaps you even wonder, "Can this marriage survive?"

I have written this book primarily for answer-seeking wives like you. While I certainly believe your husband would benefit by reading it with you, he may not. I want to help you understand why some husbands act evasively and maintain a certain distance from you. Most particularly, I want to show you what you can do to improve your emotional reactions to your husband. As you might imagine, too many wives suffer needlessly because they assume that their husbands' struggles and shortcomings are somehow their fault. The truth is, you need not carry burdens that were never yours to begin with.

As a counselor, I have dealt with many cases in which husbands inadvertently upset their wives by ignoring the meatier elements of marriage. What causes him to act that way, affecting you so strongly? Are there any hidden issues you must face as you strive so eagerly for the marital ideal? And most important, what adjustments can you make to bring peace of mind, if not a wonderful relationship, to your life?

I hope the following pages will help you answer some of these questions by broadening your understanding of how you and your spouse developed your relationship patterns and tendencies. Keep this in mind as you read: I am writing to *you*, not your mate. Focus on who you are and how your broadened mind can make you more stable and less susceptible to relational strains.

Should your spouse decide to read this book with you, let me suggest a way for you to digest its ideas together. I have included an Appendix with thoughts and questions about the material in each chapter. After each of you reads a chapter, go to its corresponding section in the Appendix and discuss your questions aloud. Use this book as a springboard to deeper intimacy and harmony. Consider establishing a time each week for your discussions.

You will notice that I have included case examples to make real the ideas in this book. For confidentiality, I have concealed the identities of the persons discussed, but the issues are very real. My desire is that you will learn by identifying with other struggling, growing people.

## chapter 1

# *P*olar-Opposite Spouses

*L*ynette Sandstrom absently twirled her glass and watched the tea and ice do their little waltz. "I don't normally throw coffee on people, Kris. What's the matter with me?"

"Oh, nuts. I forgot to bring along my sign saying 'The Doctor Is In.'" Lynette's best friend often sounded flippant, but Lynette could discuss anything with Kris, deep or shallow, and she understood. Most of all, Kris cared. "How did this all come about?"

"You know how much I got out of that women's conference. I called you Saturday night when I got home, remember?"

"Do I ever." Kris reached for her other popover. "You told me all about this one speaker who emphasized how wives can set the pace in their homes for loving and kind interaction. You must have talked about it for twenty minutes."

"Right." Lynette listened for a moment to the sparrows chirping in the trumpet vine. She loved the peace and seclusion of this little patio outside the China Pot tearoom. "Well, Sunday before church, we were having breakfast as usual. Howard was hiding behind his morning paper as usual. And I was trying to tell him about the emotional high that conference gave me. I told him

1

how I came home convinced that if I would just apply the right principles, he and I could move up to the next level and make our marriage go places!"

"So when he grunted instead of answering, you dumped the coffee in his lap." Kris slathered strawberry jam across her popover.

"How did you know he grunted?"

"Howard's a grunter. Most men are. Is that when?"

"No, but I was getting really mad. I told him *I* was the one who went to the conference. I'm *always* willing to go the extra mile for the sake of our marriage. I said it would require very little from him, except maybe a show of appreciation for my efforts. He grunted again."

"That's when you spilled the coffee."

"No, but by then I was really losing it. I reached out and shoved his paper down. Mashed it right into his oatmeal. I said, 'Talk to me!' I explained, 'I want you to discuss this with me! Ask questions. Deep things. Questions with substance!' That's getting the message across clear enough, right? He got this blank look, and then he shrugged that way he does. It means, 'Okay, dear, whatever it takes to calm you down.' Just that careless shrug makes me furious. Know what deep, substantive question he asked? 'Get any volleyball in while you were there?'" Lynette sat back with a sigh. "*That's* when I dumped my coffee on him."

## THE GREAT VOID

Lynette's frustration—and Howard's, for that matter—plays itself out in marriage all the time. The wife seeks relational and emotional depth in her marriage; the husband seeks the football scores.

To put it in Lynette's own words: "I don't know why I was so gullible as to think Howard would be enthusiastic about anything that might address our marital problems. When I try to discuss things that really matter to me his eyes instantly glaze over. As soon as he realizes that I want to talk about something more substantial than his golf game, he shuts down. Virtually nothing to say. It happens every time."

This problem seemed to touch every phase of their marriage. She and Howard, both forty-three, had been married for twenty-one years. On their anniversary, Howard gave her a car. That night as they lay in bed, Lynette observed, "This is our anniversary, and you have not once today said you loved me."

His response: "Whaddaya mean? I got you a car, didn't I?"

Does this problem sound at all familiar to you?

In many ways, an objective observer would see Lynette Sandstrom as a supermom, the most nearly perfect helpmate any man could wish for. Bubbly and expressive, never at a loss for words, Lynette enjoyed a wide circle of friends. She had long ago placed a high priority on developing *real* relationships. Her friends were loyal in return because she so willingly listened to their personal needs and encouraged them regarding the things that mattered most. No one could accuse her of not caring about people.

She was also a devoted mom. From the time her two sons, now ages seventeen and fifteen, were in grade school, Lynette made sure they were signed up for all the right athletic and church activities. She ran car pools, helped with homework, stayed plugged into their friendships, entertained guests constantly. She was quick to give Howard credit for helping with the boys' activities when he could, especially when sports were involved.

Despite all the skills and successes Lynette could claim in her extended life, she felt a great void in her relationship with Howard.

"When we met at college," she recalled, "he was friendly and liked kidding around with me. We really enjoyed each other's company. I knew from the beginning that he was the silent type. He rarely talked about things of importance, but that didn't seem to bother me then.

"I knew his dad had been hard on him. I assumed he learned to keep his thoughts to himself as protection. I was certain it would just be a matter of time before he'd realize that he could trust me and be open with me. I figured that if I'd be nurturing and enthusiastic, he couldn't help but appreciate what I had to offer and he'd eventually loosen up. Here we are, over twenty years later, and I'm still waiting for it to happen."

## Identifying the Void

Two decades is a long time to struggle with the frustrations Lynette described. What about you?

- Are you eager to be linked in a loving relationship with a man who cares about you deeply, but it's just not happening?
- Are you willing to encourage him on the deepest emotional levels, but you can't chip through the ice?
- Do you feel that despite your relatively lax expectations (i.e., making few demands), you are being taken advantage of?

In other words, does a void exist for you?

In my counseling practice I specialize in treating common emotional stresses that, if left unattended, can turn into major debilitating problems. The hurting people who come to see me are trying to cope with anger, depression, anxiety, and the like stemming from their marriage. Since these issues are usually played out in the home, I often face the task of helping people understand how their emotions relate to their unsolved marriage problems.

Over twenty-five thousand counseling sessions have shown me that the single most common marital problem I encounter is the case of an emotionally eager wife, like Lynette, whose husband will not engage with her on a deep, meaningful, and personal level. These phrases are indicators of this problem:

- "It's impossible to pin him down to any kind of real emotional commitment."
- "Just when I think we've really connected, he does something to prove he never understood a thing I said."
- "I think the guy is oblivious to my feelings."

- "What does it take to get through to him?"
- "He cares more about his work [or sports or hobbies] than he does about me."

As the relationship progresses, or rather, fails to progress, feelings of disillusionment and futility become entrenched, and faulty patterns of communication yield increasing frustration.

Failure to progress is not for lack of trying. Again, Lynette's words: "In the early years of our marriage I tried extra hard to please Howard and help him become more demonstrative. I'd pick up on the slightest hint and do whatever I could to make him feel special. Here's one instance. For several months I read the sports page while he was still in the bathroom, before he saw it. Then at breakfast, you see, I could converse with him and the boys and sound halfway intelligent. I'd toss around terms like *Hail Mary* and *wishbone formation*. He never acknowledged my efforts. He never even noticed. I felt incredibly disappointed. Betrayed. Why couldn't he appreciate me just a little bit? It wouldn't kill him.

"Sometimes I'd blow my stack and cry and scream, but that only made things worse. He'd just look at me and say, 'How can I possibly take you seriously when you act like a spoiled maniac?' Eventually, his indifference won. I feel so utterly defeated."

## The Pattern of the Void

As I consult in case after case showing similar patterns of breakdown, I see that many of these emotionally eager women have good reason to feel disappointed. Most women (not all, understand, but the vast majority) need strong, growing relationships that are openly expressed, and their husbands fail to supply that need. These wives are living with men who have unconsciously committed themselves to an evasive way of life.

The wives aren't the only ones hurt by this evasiveness. These men, unwilling to seriously explore the depths of their own emotional needs, perch securely atop their own little time bombs. As frustration and confusion mount, something will eventually blow.

Most of them, though, would rather eat snake eggs than admit, "You know, I need to find out why I act the way I do. Surely there are some solid adjustments I could make in order to be a better husband."

Yeah, sure. So instead, they plod along year after year in a cautious rut of unconcern or oblivion. They know instinctively that deep probing might hurt. As long as the distant relational patterns they've devised continue to protect them from the ugly introspection their wives seem to dwell on, they don't have to take a hard, painful, inward look. Of course, they also lose all the excellent benefits that come from introspection.

In the meantime, their wives are going nuts trying to find some way to change these guys from brick walls into sofa cushions; you know—softies who raise the comfort level by giving a little. The wives try one method after another, such as Lynette's attempt to bone up on the sports her husband loves, to force deeper personal communication. Their attempts flop. As the defeats pile up, their emotional stability goes straight down the tubes. That's when they come to see me. "I'd have better luck filling the bathtub by dipping water with a spoon. It'd be more productive too. What am I going to do with this guy?"

## COPING WITH THE VOID

If at all possible, I include husbands in my counseling sessions. You'd be surprised how often these undemonstrative men are looking, deep inside, for a way to jump-start their marriages. At least at an unexplored level, they are begging for someone to show them a better way to relate to their wives. In these cases, the potential for counseling success is very strong. I can show spouses the best method to address their unique relational needs, and the lessons will probably "take."

When the husband, however, is unwilling to participate in counseling, the wife still has some excellent options. Her spouse may cling to stubborn, evasive patterns of relating, but she can make improvements in two general areas.

1. Have you noticed that in our culture, the burden of a relationship often falls on the woman? The woman is expected to "make it work." If a man remains faithful, he gets the credit; if he strays, it's somehow her fault, at least in part. When a relationship unravels, the greater share of the blame ends on her doorstep. Counseling, however, can help a woman learn what lies behind the scenes of her husband's personality, what makes him do what he does. With that knowledge in hand, she can come to realize that her husband's behavior is not her fault after all.

2. The woman can examine the ways in which she reacts to her husband. From there she can figure out better ways of relating that will cause her less stress and personal frustration. Then, even if he never improves his behavior, she can still enjoy improved personal stability. She can be happier.

As you may have guessed, Lynette arranged to see me after the coffee episode. Caring as she was, Kris is a stockbroker, not a therapist. In fact, it was Kris who suggested Lynette seek help in coping with Howard's obtuseness.

When I begin counseling with a client, the first visit is a get-acquainted session in which the client describes the problem he or she (since it's Lynette, I'll stick with "she" from now on) perceives. We get to know each other. Then, as we progress from week to week, the fabric of the client's relationships unrolls and we dig out the underlying causes of the surface problems.

Even in this first session, Lynette came across as a classy woman. Usually, "bubbly" and "classy" don't go together well, but in her, they melded beautifully. She dressed well and groomed herself well without appearing overly made-up. She didn't sit in chairs; she draped herself within them, legs gracefully crossed, arms at ease. A native Texan, she spoke English with a soft, delicate southern accent.

That accent seemed to add poignancy to her opening statement. "I don't know what made me do it. I am not a person given to violence. The coffee, I mean. It wasn't hot. Lukewarm. I'd been sipping at it for fifteen minutes. It certainly wasn't to hurt him. I'd never do that. It was to—I guess, to wake him up. That sounds so strange. Am I crazy?"

"Not strange at all. It's an excellent insight."

"And I'm genuinely sorry that Howard refuses to join me in this. He insists that he's already doing the best he can, and you can't do any more than that. If I did force him here, he'd just resist everything. It would be a waste of time and money."

"Another sharp insight. You can't change him from the outside. But you can change you from the inside. You can also change the patterns of relating to him that frustrate you so much. Once you understand what's going on, you'll be able to control your own emotions better. Sound like a goal to work for?"

Lynette very nearly dissolved into tears right there. "After twenty-one years of this, what do you think?"

## Identifying Patterns

The first step toward improving one's relationship is to understand what constitutes patterns in marriages that can, frankly, be emotionally abusive.

It sounds so far as if I've been painting the nasty old husbands as villains. That's not true in the least. Most of these men have perfectly honorable intentions and would never try to hurt their wives. But even though they usually do not set out to harm, it happens all the same. The problem lies in the way most (not *all* by any means!) men approach life. As a general rule, men are less naturally inclined than women to address personal or sensitive subjects. This isn't simply fear of pain. They really aren't as interested. They have a natural tendency to bypass the lengthy processing that is so necessary to intimate personal interchanges and skip straight to the solution.

Lynette's eyes went wide. "That's it exactly! I'll describe a problem to Howard that I want to talk about, and he'll say something like, 'A problem, huh? Well, here's the answer.' End of discussion."

When the wife seeks greater depth than simply problem-options-solution and presses to explore the emotional side of an issue or its ramifications, the man's frustration kicks in. "We've already handled the problem; therefore, it doesn't exist anymore; so what is it with this woman?" To him, detailed processing is useless, perhaps even inane.

He then—and this is a key—begins looking for ways to end his participation in his wife's processing. He may withdraw or try to put her back onto a path of logic or perhaps even explode. The explosion, you see, is a diversion, a distraction—in essence, a change of subject. Changing the subject is another often-used way out of processing. He is guided by the dread of having to spend any more time than is necessary to dwell on her emotional needs, for he almost never sees them as needs.

Women generally experience feelings and emotions more intensely than do men, mostly because they allow themselves to. A wife lets emotions run their course even as the husband is trying to stuff them, to get rid of them, for he sees them as anti-productive. Let me emphasize that there is no right-and-wrong about having strong emotions or even, to some extent, downplaying them. But because she recognizes and even nurtures her emotional side, the wife can enjoy life in its richest, fullest dimension.

Relationships and family connections are the most important ingredients in most wives' lives. By their very nature, close relationships generate strong emotions. The wife can inadvertently create problems when she so craves emotional connections that she loses the ability to respond with reason or calm. She may become anxious; she certainly becomes angry. Not to put too fine a point on it, but hers is an *insistent* anger whereas his is a *resistant* anger.

The woman locked into these patterns can cry and complain that she feels unloved. She has such a powerful need to feel understood and cherished at an emotional level that she becomes greatly disillusioned when external signs of that understanding are nonexistent. To illustrate, let me introduce Gary and Ruth.

Gary and Ruth. What a pair! A dyslexic high school dropout, huge, hulking Gary couldn't discern *lain* from *nail,* but he sure could push dirt. In ten years, he turned a single, leased bulldozer into a million-dollar enterprise employing nine drivers and two full-time mechanics. He bought that initial bulldozer from the rental company and enshrined it in the front yard of his business office. He threatened to have it bronzed, but Ruth put her foot down. (Incidentally, the fact that he outweighed her by almost a hundred pounds didn't seem to make any difference in the marriage at all). Ruth, petite and perky, graduated with all A's and dreamed of becoming a CPA. She married Gary and became a mother instead, but she took accounting courses on the side. She still kept Gary's books, although the load was really too heavy for one person.

Now they sat in my office intent on damage control, trying to patch their latest marital rift. The tiff had happened the night before.

Ruth opened with, "All I asked him to do was mow the lawn and fix the sliding patio screen door. That door has been jamming for a month. Every time the kids go in or out, it gets hung up. And the grass was tall enough for a rabbit to hide in without ducking. Oh, and the kids were at their youth group, so I asked him to help with the dishes. The kids usually help."

I asked, "Do you two have an understanding of some sort, who does which chores?"

Ruth grimaced. "Come to think of it, yeah. We sure do. The rule is, 'Let Ruthie do it.' Gary doesn't lift a finger."

The scowl on Gary's face suggested to me that this was not the first time they had talked about this. "Look. I work a ten-hour day, sometimes six days a week out in the weather. Real cold and real hot is murder, you know. I finally get home, she wants me to work another ten."

Ruth turned on him. "Look yourself, Pal. I spend at least eight hours a day trying to untangle your lousy record-keeping and make the books balance right. And that's not including all the stuff the kids constantly need. The least you can do is mow the lawn."

As the acrimonious debate progressed, I could tell that Gary's lawn-mowing job was indeed the least he could do. He skipped the patch behind the garage and didn't bother to trim along the flower beds. And the screen door still jammed.

"Hey," he protested. "I ran WD-40 along the track. That door is floating in lubricant."

"Big deal. It still jams. If it was simply a matter of lubricating it, I would have done it. The frame is bent where Tiger kicked it. All the WD-40 in the world isn't going to help that."

And on and on it went. To summarize, after doing the bare minimum, Gary plopped down in front of the TV. When Ruth started raining on him about dishes and screen doors, he nodded, "Yeah, yeah," got up, and walked out of the room. Thirty minutes later Ruth went looking for him and found him napping on the bed. On the bedspread. Without removing his shoes.

Now she clouded up and *really* rained all over him. He announced that he was done talking to her and clammed up. She substituted weeping for sleeping through most of that night. In my office, the clouds of war still had not dispersed.

Waving a hand the size of as tennis racket, Gary offered, "I hate it when Ruthie bosses me and tries to force me into doing favors for her. I pull my share of the load. If I wanted a boss, I'd work for Hastings Construction. I sure didn't marry to get one."

Who had the legitimate complaint here? It doesn't matter. What matters is the pattern they were following, almost as if they were enslaved to a script. She vented her anger. He responded with what we call passive aggression—that is, being obstructive and uncooperative (the poorly done lawn and door jobs were the visible external evidence). She pushed. He withdrew, to the point of going to sleep. Even angrier now, she pushed harder, which caused him to evade the situation openly, stuffing the conflict and simply refusing to deal with any aspect of it.

Crying, Ruth wailed, "He does this stuff to me all the time! I can never count on him. Sometimes he can be the sweetest husband and I think everything's terrific. Then, he'll pull stunts like this, and it takes me days to get over it. When is he ever going to be consistent?"

Actually, Gary was being consistent—consistently evasive.

Evasive husbands invent a broad range of behaviors for avoiding the in-depth discussions they see as useless and potentially harmful: the silent treatment, pretended agreement, constant forgetfulness, procrastination, laziness, temper outbursts, workaholism, undue attention to a hobby or sport, and in general merely being unavailable. The evasive man may tune out. He might say whatever he thinks his wife wants to hear at that moment, to prevent the boat from rocking, you see, and harbors no intention of actually following through.

To counter evasiveness, the emotionally eager wife will be prone toward responses such as crying, persuading, calling friends for support, acting moody, repeating the same requests, accusing, and giving up.

Once the cycle gets going it can be difficult to break.

## Factors Behind the Pattern

In my practice I see seven factors that are very common in marriages affected by the evasive and the emotionally eager relationship patterns. As we examine them, you will see that this tug-of-war is not confined to a few aberrant households. It is widespread. I find this tension in the homes of driven, success-oriented people and in laid-back, take-it-easy relationships. Some of the participants have a history of poor relations with others, while some can point to great popularity with others.

If your husband will join you in the awareness process, that's great! Use the information provided as a springboard for healthy, honest discussion. If he will not, and many won't, choose to make yourself aware of what's happening and grow anyway. One person working toward a healthy style of relating is better than no one at all taking steps.

Let's look at the seven indicators, using Lynette and Howard as the examples.

**1. Communication is reduced to power plays.** If nothing else, evasive behavior creates a feeling of power. Somewhere in Howard's past, this thought took root: "People would love to tell me what to do, but I'm not going to let it happen." Call it independence, or call it stubbornness. Howard's underlying attitude is very common. Howard will interpret Lynette's needs as an effort to control him, something he will not tolerate. Sensing his resistance, emotionally eager Lynette works even harder to force him to understand and meet her needs. This renewed effort requires increased resistance. The power play is on.

This concept of control and power-wielding can take some strange twists, and the people involved usually do not see it for what it is. For instance, Lynette did not see her set-to with Howard regarding the washer repairman as a power play at all.

Lynette described the incident. "I called the repairman out because the agitator wasn't—" She frowned a moment. "You know, agitating. Incidentally, it costs thirty-five dollars just to watch him walk in the door for a house call. Anyway, he gave it a few twists and said, 'You're loading your machine too full. Don't put so much in and it'll work okay.'

"Well, I wasn't loading it any more than I always did, and it didn't work with half loads either, and I told him so. 'No, no, no, you're loading it too full. Thirty-five bucks, please.'

"So I called Howard and asked him to talk to the guy. Howard said, 'I'm too busy. It's your problem. You take care of it.'

"I said, 'But he won't listen to me! Maybe he'll listen to you. Please talk to him.'

"And Howard says, 'Can't. Too busy.' Then I broke into tears and he hung up. And that was that. The washer repairman went home with thirty-five dollars he didn't earn, my washer still doesn't work, and I'm so mad and frustrated with Howard that I can't bear to look at him."

Lynette was too emotionally embroiled with the problem to see the power play at work here, but I think you the reader can analyze it. Not being taken seriously is a problem that more women than men face. Howard probably never ran into that problem himself and so he discounted it. You tell the repairman what's wrong, he fixes it or tells you how to get around it. What's so tough about that? Lynette was obviously making another mountain out of still another molehill, trying to coerce Howard into doing something he didn't feel like doing. Howard saw the incident as a power play on Lynette's part. It was also a power play on his. He could control Lynette's situation because she had virtually handed it over to him. And so he did.

Understand none of this was a considered, thought-out action on the part of either spouse. It was all going on pretty much below conscious level, as are so many control issues and power plays.

Evasive husbands, with their intense fear of being dominated, can turn the simplest request into a major battle over control. Quite possibly this fear has legitimate roots, if the man's past is scarred with bad experiences. You'll recall that Lynette referred to the tough time Howard had growing up under domineering parents.

If the emotionally eager wife responds with her own overbearing style instead of understanding his fear of being controlled, she does the very thing that makes matters worse. She speaks coercively.

Perversely, even a caring husband derives a certain subconscious satisfaction when he witnesses the wife in great emotional distress. The underlying thought: *You see? I do have power! I can control her emotions, and that's not an easy thing to do. My tactics worked.* The more the wife registers anger or anxiety or futility, the more likely the evasive husband will continue to respond with power tactics. His urgent, compelling need to keep the upper hand is satisfied. And I repeat, this is not necessarily deliberate. Usually, it is all going on in the darkest caverns of the mind.

**2. *He avoids commitment and personal accountability.*** A common complaint I hear from emotionally eager wives is that they cannot get a solid commitment to anything. Their man is hard to pin down.

"Oh, heavens, yes!" Lynette rolled her eyes. "I'll say, 'Let's go out to Porky's for ribs tonight. It's too hot to cook.' Porky's is Howard's favorite place, but what does he say? 'Let's wait and see.' Not no. Not yes. I ask him to stop at the dry cleaners for his dress pants and he says, 'I have to see how my day goes first.'" In frustration, Lynette finished with, "For crying out loud! It's his pants!"

Remember that evasive husbands unconsciously lust for power. They must maintain control. So it isn't hard to see why they don't want to be held accountable to specific plans. They have confused *commitment* with *enslavement* or *coercion* and wrongly assume the words mean much the same thing. They see simple requests, then, as attempts at coercion, and they circumvent them by remaining vague.

Time after time I hear these telltale statements reflecting the commitment problem:

- "I've given up asking him to help with family projects because I never know if he'll follow through on what he says."
- "He tells me he'll be home by six o'clock, but I know that means at least six-thirty."
- "I've decided if I want things done right around here I'll have to do them myself."
- "My husband's promises carry little weight these days."

These men realize that accountability requires a certain amount of vulnerability, and that scares them. Clear communication, self-revelation, and openness: These qualities could boomerang on them, they fear. The evasive person also fears that his good nature will be taken advantage of, so he plays it safe by revealing the least amount that he can about his plans, his preferences, his feelings.

Although these men would never admit it even to themselves, they have made a commitment to dishonesty. Sometimes blatant lying is involved, as when a man says he will do something, knowing full well that he will not. But usually this dishonesty is more subtle. Without openly lying, these men try to create an illusion of cooperation when in fact they inwardly hope to blaze their own trails independently of their mates' plans.

With this fear of accountability, these men fuel the wives' worst fears of marital isolation. The men do whatever they must to keep a safe distance—exactly the opposite of what the emotionally eager wives are seeking. The men keep their feelings well hidden; the wives want feelings brought into view. The men think they dare not expose their preferences lest they be denied (in other words, the woman controls the situation through the power of choice). The women want more than anything else to know what their men want.

Needless to say, this factor of poor accountability works against the success of any relationship, for a thriving marriage needs sharing and openness in order to be truly fused into a unit.

*3. Leadership roles are confused.* With all this control jockeying and poor accountability, the third factor in these conflicted marriages isn't hard to see: badly defined leadership roles. The evasive husband prefers to hold back and sidestep situations that will bring his wife's criticism to bear, and that includes certain situations where his leadership would be expected. He may even coyly set her up to take the heat. That, you see, is real control! Have any of these scenarios happened in your home?

- A child makes a request that Dad knows should be turned down, so he says, "Why don't you ask your mother?" Let her be the ogre who denies the child's wants.
- The husband hears someone reprimand his wife. This might

be a stranger in public or his own mother in private. Instead of standing up for his wife, he remains silent even though he knows his wife feels abandoned.

- Your husband believes differently from his extended family about a sensitive subject (religion, politics, business). Instead of expressing his belief and thereby sticking his neck out (making a commitment to an idea, actually), he waits for someone to ask the wife, "What do you think?"
- It's his wife's birthday. Instead of giving her a well-thought-out gift, he says, "Why don't you go buy yourself something nice? It's on me."

These husbands know that the more leadership they exert, the more controversy they may encounter. It works that way in politics; it must work that way in marriage. Notice that the power plays are still going on. But here we're talking about open, visible leadership. Being chronic conflict avoiders, these men prefer to lie low and stay out of the fray. In the battle of the sexes, it's a good way to keep your head from being shot off. They falsely assume that openness invites problems.

It's that don't-rock-the-boat thing again. Unfortunately, by backing away from the leadership role, these men are sacrificing the family's long-term needs—a stable leader—for the short-term goal of peace-for-the-moment.

Interestingly, in many cases, men who back out of the leadership role in personal and family matters are anything *but* weak in business pursuits or civic projects.

Lynette would be the first to agree. "Howard is a real hustler when it comes to keeping his company competitive. Innovative. Right up front. And you should see him when it comes to organizing his Lion's Club's eye bank project. But try to get him to back me up when I have to discipline the boys. They're getting too big to handle, and I have no support from Howard whatsoever. It scares me to death that the boys might make too many wrong choices, and he won't step in until it's too late."

*4. Relationship is secondary to performance.* Human beings err, make occasional wrong choices, and are occasionally selfish. In healthy marriages, the partners recognize this fact and allow plenty of room for open conflict resolution. Emotionally eager wives would welcome the chance to discuss problems. But because the evasive husband prefers to minimize his own emotional vulnerability, he customarily runs from the threat of having to struggle with emotions. Logic tells us that if a man is running away from something, he is also running toward something else. What is it that men run toward to avoid personal interactions? *Performance.*

Now, as a very general rule, men are performance-oriented anyway. Whereas women enjoy the process of doing something, men want to reach the goal as quickly and efficiently as possible and go on to something else. (Again I remind you, there are plenty of exceptions to this.) You'll recall that on her twenty-first anniversary, Lynette missed being told "I love you." Howard figured giving her the car said it well enough. In his eyes, the act was sufficient and replaced a verbal expression.

There's a downside, though. Being performance-oriented allows men to sidestep personal responsibilities while simultaneously giving the appearance of being very responsible.

For instance:

- The wife complains, "You never take the time out to check on your parents' health problems. You always leave it up to me to make the phone call." To which he replies, "Haven't you forgotten that I've been sitting here at the computer figuring out this month's budget?"
- The wife tells her husband he needs to spend more time one-on-one with their daughter, so he agrees to coach her soccer team. Notice that he still doesn't take out personal time for *her.*
- The wife asks for more time just so the two of them can talk about personal matters. He replies, "I'd love to, Hon, but I've got to stay late at work and finish this report."

As a general rule, men tend to gain greater satisfaction from achievement than from personally revealing moments. That is not to say this is absolute, but it is the norm. In counseling one afternoon, Lynette related, "I've asked Howard dozens of times recently to take some time out just to talk with me, not just about problems but about us. He always has an excuse why he can't. Then last week his brother called because he needed some help building a shed in his backyard, and Howard gave up three evenings in a row to help him out. I feel just plain old abandoned."

Sure Howard found time for his brother but not his wife. His brother asked for performance. Lynette wanted to spend time "just" relating. She was trying to connect with him on a level that did not register. Commonly, evasive men will not mind giving time to an activity such as yard work, fishing, a project at the church. It's familiar turf. They already know how to do those things. They'll see a nice, neat, tucked-in end to it and, ideally, fruit from their labors—a trimmed-up yard, the new church fence, perhaps a fish or two . . . something. But relationships require *being* not *doing*, an unsettling concept for many men.

**5. Sexual relating is out of sync.** Happy, growing marriages are typified by reasonable sexual communication. Although frequency is not the chief concern (some couples are satisfied with twice monthly sex, some enjoy it several times a week), union occurs frequently enough to remind the spouses of their love and commitment to each other. Sex is a means of maintaining secure bonding.

For evasive men, however, sex is intended not for bonding but for physical satisfaction and—here it is again—control. Who's in the driver's seat?

At one extreme, the evasive man abstains for long periods of time, showing virtually no interest at all in his wife sexually. He knows sex can bring out tender sharing, something he prefers to avoid. He determines that it is easier to deny the pleasures of sexual relating in order to avoid emotional intimacy. I have heard numerous accounts from women who are eager to be sexually involved with their husbands but are rebuffed for six months at a time, a year, or longer.

The more common extreme has the evasive man showing little tenderness during the waking hours. When bedtime comes, his engine turns on, and he gets his satisfaction from his wife. Then he slips back into his comfortable shell. He may even turn on at two o'clock in the morning, make his move, then go back to sleep. This approach to sex neatly minimizes emotional intimacy without minimizing the feel-good experience. The wife's emotions are hardly considered.

The emotionally eager wife, then, develops conflicting feelings about marital sex. Part of her wants it and sees it as a wonderful communication time, but she is afraid of the hurt that comes as she senses her husband is merely after physical relief. Some of these wives will nonetheless remain sexually willing, thinking it can open up the husband and create the connection they so strongly desire. Others, tired of the game, will shut down. They have decided that if the husband wants to turn sex into a purely physical release, he will have to learn to respect her unwillingness to be used for this narrow purpose.

Often, if this conflict goes on long enough, one spouse or the other may opt for an outside form of sexual satisfaction: an affair, pornography, or flirtations outside marriage. *Either* spouse can feel such strong disappointment as to be abnormally vulnerable to temptation.

**6. *Personal insights are unequal.*** The more you know, the more you know you don't know. Who has been able to say, "I've arrived at the summit of knowledge! I've solved all my problems." Even if someone could honestly say that, there are still those nagging little errors human beings keep making, mistakes born not of ignorance but of humanity.

Healthy people not only admit the need for improvement, they welcome the challenge. Well, anyway, most of the time. They are certainly open to others' input. The fact that you are reading this book indicates that you are too. Growing people are willing to absorb insights and information. They actively seek out truth.

Evasive people are not inclined toward insight and awareness. Apart from the fact that it's too much trouble for what you get out of it, the evasive husband really isn't interested in being challenged on the personal, philosophical level. That makes him too vulnerable. He wants the comfortable routines, the level keel, putting little or no thought into the whys of life.

Gary, the massive bulldozer operator who could probably bench-press his bulldozer, put it this way when I asked him to explain his thoughts. "What difference does it make? Why should I go all through that? None of it amounts to a hill of beans when I'm out on a tractor. Learning?" He spat—fortunately a dry gesture of contempt. "I spent ten years in school being told I was a dummy. I'd learn if only I would apply myself. When I tested out dyslexic, I got this routine, 'Look at all the famous people who were dyslexic and they managed anyway.' Hey. I'm good at what I do, and I make good money. You can shove your challenge-to-grow."

Okay, so I challenged him to at least grasp a couple of the concepts that could eliminate some of his tensions with Ruth. That classified as useful information, didn't it?

Nope. Said Gary, "I can communicate just fine. Ask any of the guys who work for me. I can communicate with Ruthie when I want to. She just has to learn when to leave me alone."

Of course, in Gary's book, when he actually wanted to communicate above the most basic level with Ruth was "never," and when she was supposed to leave him alone was "all the time."

The emotionally eager wives are usually the type who devour self-help books, enjoy stimulating philosophical discussions, flock to seminars. They invite growth. They like being challenged about what can be done to create a fuller life and why they need to make the needed adjustments. Result: They grow and expand intellectually as their husbands tune in still another football game.

This eagerness does not always translate into significant change. Because of the wife's tendency to play off her husband's behavior—reacting instead of proacting—this woman eventually loses heart as she realizes that her efforts are not being matched by his. She begins to perceive that she's outgrowing him. I've seen many of these wives become increasingly agitated or collapse in despair or depression. Either way, the woman ought to press forward, gaining insight, regardless of her mate's lack of interest.

**7. Both sides feel victimized.** Evasive husbands subconsciously live with a philosophy of "You leave me alone, I'll leave you alone, and we'll get along just fine." The fewer challenges they encounter, the less conflict they experience, and the better they feel. The problem is that their spouses by nature yearn for a far more intimate pattern of relating. The wife launches her various attempts to get the intimacy and depth she craves, protesting or cajoling or simply acting unhappy. The husband, turned off by his wife's prodding, sulks and wonders, "Why do I have to live with this kind of stuff? She's crabby for no good reason." Either unwilling or unable to grasp that he is contributing to the problem, he sees himself as a victim of unreasonableness. Victims are not cheerful people. The tenor—the feel, if you will—of the household nose-dives as anger and sadness feed on each other.

The emotionally eager wife feels just as victimized. "When is all this misery going to end? Look what he's doing to my life. It's sterile! Going nowhere. Emotionally zip. When will he ever wake up, or is it always going to be this miserable?"

When Lynette's friend Kris phoned with simply, "Popover time," Lynette jumped at the chance. They met at the China Pot as usual. Settled at their table on the patio, the flowers whispering sweet nothings overhead, Lynette confided, "I'm going crazy. I'm much more verbal than Howard. If I feel something, I can't hold it in very long. I have to talk about it."

"I've noticed."

"Well, so do you. And when I try to tell him what's happening, he tunes me out. Bang! Just like that. It's like talking to a fence post, only the fence post doesn't sulk and act like it's being abused."

"He doesn't like criticism."

"Who does? But how else can I get through to him?"

"Dump any more coffee on him?"

Lynette snorted. "That doesn't work either. It just makes more laundry for me." She paused to work on her popover a moment. "He uses anything I try to say as an excuse to retreat and feel sorry for himself because he has it so rough."

Kris leaned forward, tête-à-tête. "Know what I think?"

"What?"

"I think you have a problem." Kris extended her hand, palm up. "That'll be five cents, please."

Lynette bit into her popover, glum as the public hangman. "It's not worth two."

In a sense, there is truth to each mate's feeling of victimization. Both spouses can point to evidence that this marriage has become something of a raw deal. Both can show legitimate ways in which the other spouse is contributing to the problem. Neither sees the whole picture. When either of them places all blame on the other partner, the "I'm a victim" attitude has gone too far.

Once this evasive pattern has become entrenched in a marriage, it is tempting to place full blame onto the shoulders of the husband who resists deep relating. Let's say that, in certain instances, it's true. He does need to change his ways of relating to his wife. His evasiveness damages and even destroys his position of influence in his own home. After all, God did not place us here on earth to avoid each other. We were made to relate first to God, then with family and friends.

Evasive behaviors are damaging, not just to the wife but to the husband as well, preventing him from knowing the satisfaction God intended for him. In the chapters to follow, I will offer some practical ways in which he can identify and understand why he behaves as he does. And I will describe alternatives that will ultimately prove much more rewarding.

The emotionally eager wife, though, needs to be aware that she, too, can feed the very patterns of behavior she dislikes. It will benefit her immensely to see how, being too emotionally reactive, she gives her husband the very excuse he needs to remain evasive. There are ways for her to respond more constructively to her husband, contributing to solutions rather than problems. That tense atmosphere in Lynette's home, in Gary and Ruth's home, and in yours can be eased and brightened. There are good ways to build a more rewarding partnership for both partners. We've seen the problem. Let's look now at solutions.

## chapter 2

# Starting the Awareness Process

*T*he Olympic weightlifting team aren't the only folks who have perfected the clean and jerk. Ruth Sweeney used it all the time on her patio screen door. You clean the runner and then simultaneously lift and jerk it to get it closed. Anger boiled up every time she had to put down whatever she was carrying so that she had both hands free to shut the blasted door.

She closed the offending screen door for the umpteenth time that morning and froze in her tracks. "Aaron Lewis Sweeney! We leave for Sunday school in five minutes and you're in cutoffs. Hike up those stairs and get dressed for church!"

Her elder son (Tiger when he wasn't being scolded with his full name) gave her an impatient you-don't-understand look. "I'm not going. Rico has to get the blade repaired before tomorrow, so he's working overtime today and I get to help him."

Ruth scowled at him, arms folded. "Oh really! Number one, you are eleven years old, and you're too young to be messing around the heavy equipment. And the road grader is the heaviest.

No. Number two. You will go to Sunday school like the rest of this family. Number—"

"Dad's not going. How come he can stay and fix the blade and I can't? He said I could." Tiger's voice was taking on the whine that always accompanied his sales pitches. "Dad says I ought to learn mechanics."

"You ought to learn Scripture too. Get upstairs."

"Go ask Dad. He'll tell you. I can stay."

Too furious to speak, Ruth pointed up the stairs.

Tiger stood a moment, obviously weighing options. With exaggerated reluctance and vivid pouting, he slogged up the stairs.

Ruth lifted and jerked the screen door open and stomped out without closing it. Fire in her eye and spring in her step, she crossed the lawn—it needed mowing again—and roared out across the equipment yard. "Gary? Gary!"

Their mechanic, Rico Morales, straddled the drive shaft of the Caterpillar blade. He smiled at her, more an "Oh-Oh!" grin than a "Hi there!" one, and busied himself with the linkage.

Ruth addressed the legs and shoes emerging from behind the front wheels, the only part of Gary she could see. "Why did you tell Tiger he could stay home from church? What's the matter with you, anyway?!"

"Hey, Ruthie. I remember when I was that age. You can't force him to go and expect him to get anything out of it. It's a stage he's going through. He'll outgrow it."

"Gary—"

"I was the same way when I was his age."

"You still are!"

## THE EVASIVENESS INVENTORY

Ask Gary Sweeney where the problem was in his marriage, and he'd point to his wife. "Ruthie. Always on somebody's case about something—usually mine." Ask Ruth, and she'd point to Gary's evasive behavior that drove her absolutely crazy. Not the least of that behavior was subtly turning the kids against her in an it's-us-versus-Mom attitude.

Pointing fingers may be satisfying to some. When one lays blame, one feels that he is getting to the core of a problem. But laying blame is not fruitful. So as a first step toward a fruitful resolution to conflict, let's identify the extent to which you and your spouse both contribute to marital tension in your household.

I'm making several assumptions here based on my experience with thousands of people. Remember that they are generalizations with many exceptions. We will assume, based on the assumption that you've read this far, that you believe evasiveness is causing friction in your family. Or perhaps you know a friend or relative with problems, and this book describes their symptoms. As a second assumption we will identify the husband as the evasive partner seeking to avoid in-depth intimacy and growth. We will assume the wife is the partner seeking greater emotional satisfaction. Certainly, in many troubled marriages the roles are reversed, but this second assumption is true in the majority of cases.

Let's identify the problem from two angles. First, if the evasive spouse permits, we'll help that person measure how strongly he frustrates the flow of marital communication. Then we'll examine the wife's emotionally eager pattern. Notice that neither person is off the hook. Both play a role.

## Inventorying the Extent of the Problem

(Remember our assumptions. If you think you might be the evasive one, adjust the questions accordingly.)

Check the responses that frequently apply to your spouse:

____ 1. He really doesn't like talking extensively with me about emotional or personal issues.

____ 2. Rather than admitting his real feelings, he just says, "I'm doing fine." That way, people won't bother him.

___    3. As I confront my husband about a problem, I can tell he's thinking of his rebuttal and not of my problem.

___    4. Sometimes he says what he thinks I want to hear just to keep peace.

___    5. There are times when he deliberately avoids me so we won't get caught in an argument or a drawn-out discussion.

___    6. I know he feels resentment now and then, but that doesn't mean he'll talk about the problem. He says talk wouldn't do any good anyway.

___    7. If he does express irritation, he keeps bringing up past events.

___    8. It's very important for him to appear unrattled in public.

___    9. He has his ideas of how life should unfold, and nobody is going to tell him what to do.

___    10. When he thinks I talk too much, he withdraws or clams up.

___    11. More than once I've told him that he's stubborn.

___    12. Many times, his goal seems to be simply keeping me from becoming upset. He says he'd be happy if I would learn to not get angry or bothered.

___    13. He has strong opinions, but he won't discuss or modify them. I believe he holds them too rigidly.

___    14. I am annoyed when he gets totally lost in some activity such as watching TV, puttering on the computer, or tinkering around in the garage.

___    15. He rarely or never admits to faults and cannot seem to say, "I'm sorry."

___    16. He avoids making specific commitments to my requests, sidestepping the issue by saying something like, "I'll have to think about it."

___    17. When I'm upset, he distances himself and won't help me sift things out.

18. He pursues behaviors or activities that do not include me.

___ **19.** He's not the type to read self-help books. He thinks "eagerly searching for the ingredients of emotional health" is nonproductive.

___ **20.** Deep, probing discussions annoy him.

No one can read the above items without checking at least a few of them. Every one of us can have moments of withdrawal or emotional shutdown. Sometimes it is normal not to want to be heavily drawn into personal or spirited exchanges. If you checked fewer than five, you two probably get into enough lively discussions and personal stimulation that your level of communication is adequate. If these are balanced by appropriate quiet moments and reflection, you are likely to feel satisfied.

If you checked between five and nine, there's a good chance your spouse contributes to some extent to marital tensions by being evasive or noncommunicative. He could probably be a lot more sensitive to what you say and need. You face an interesting challenge but not a daunting one.

If you checked ten or more items, serious evasive traits probably need to be rooted out if your marriage is to be improved—perhaps even salvaged.

Let me here insert a message to the husband:

> *Whether or not you think your present attitude and level of communication should suffice, it doesn't. You cannot continue saying that you don't want to discuss personal matters. That attitude is already greatly costing your marriage and could indeed ruin it. You're going to have to bite the bullet and start talking about the subjects your spouse claims are needs, whether you think they are her needs or not. Take heart. I've seen people with evasive traits make great strides without suffering unduly. You can do it!*

It might be instructive to play turnabout. If he will, let your spouse take the above inventory, answering as he sees you. You'll each be surprised at the different perceptions.

If your marriage has any of the seven signs mentioned in the first chapter, you already know that the two of you are moving in opposite directions. The relationship can easily deteriorate into a frustrating stalemate as each partner exhibits ever more extreme reactions to the other.

"Yeah, I'll agree with that." Ruth Sweeney sat in my office, looking ragged and tired. "I don't know how much longer we're going to keep on this way before something snaps."

"Snaps. As in a rubber band stretched too tight?"

"That's it exactly. Gary is so plumb certain he's a decent husband and doesn't need any improvement. He figures as long as he puts food on the table and gas in car, I shouldn't expect anything else. Sex now and then, of course. He used to fight when I got mad. Now he just climbs into this shell and pulls the lid down. It's like dealing with a box tortoise. You know it's in there somewhere, but you can't get to it."

"You've been married twelve years."

"Thirteen come May. We got married the week before I graduated."

"Three children."

She nodded.

"You have too much invested in your relationship to throw it away. Ever take those tests in checkout counter magazines?"

She smiled suddenly and looked almost ashamed. "Yeah, all the time. Just for fun."

"Let's do another one. This one you won't find in magazines, and it may be far more revealing and helpful."

This one measures the extent of an emotionally eager wife's responses to her husband's evasiveness.

## The Emotionally Eager Inventory

Not only does the evasive partner need to identify and alter his discussion tactics, the emotionally eager spouse must also recognize the ways in which she may be making matters worse. In a typical case, by identifying and altering her own behavior, she can bring about a degree of improvement.

To analyze whether you tend to respond to your husband in ways that make a bad thing worse, check the following items that fairly frequently apply to you.

____ 1. In personal discussions, especially regarding marriage, I have to make a point repeatedly to be sure it registers. It seems like it just bounces off him.

____ 2. My husband says I nag and complain too much.

____ 3. I often find myself asking rhetorical questions that reflect my exasperation. Examples: "Why do you have to be so stubborn?" "What is wrong with you?"

____ 4. My good mood disappears when he is insensitive or inattentive.

____ 5. It really eats away at me when he doesn't follow through with a promise.

____ 6. I have a lot of expectations that he seems unable to maintain.

____ 7. I really enjoy connecting with friends and family in stimulating discussion.

____ 8. I don't always know how to end an argument gracefully.

____ 9. Most of my satisfaction comes from relationships as opposed to projects or achievements.

____ 10. When I'm emotionally excited it's hard for me to allow others the time to think through their feelings.

____ 11. Others tell me that there are times when worry or insecurity become too prominent in my personality.

____ 12. It's hard for me to accept the fact that he can be so different from me.

____ 13. I don't usually hide my moods as well as he does.

____ 14. Although I know I shouldn't, I sometimes act as if it's my job to show him the appropriate way to think or feel.

____ 15. People get on my nerves when they fail to follow through on what they're supposed to do.

_____ **16.** I feel like a hired servant in my own home. That bothers me.

_____ **17.** I often feel that my deepest emotional needs are left dangling.

_____ **18.** When I really want to talk about something, it's hard for me just to keep quiet.

_____ **19.** Among my friends I'm known as someone who can laugh and put people at ease.

_____ **20.** I suppose you could say that I try too hard to make my marriage become closer to ideal than it ever will be.

Because no two people mesh perfectly at an emotional level, it is normal to feel distant or misunderstood at times. In fact, if you checked less than five items, you may be numb to the emotional side of life to an unhealthy degree. You could benefit by searching out and recognizing the legitimate emotions that are part of being human.

If you checked between five and nine items, you may be fairly easily influenced by your spouse's behaviors. You've probably been involved in a few more emotional disputes than you would like, but still, that's pretty normal. Keep up your willingness to talk about emotions, but pay attention to his responses. Are you pulling your mate too far from his comfort zones?

If you checked ten or more items, your emotions are probably too strongly tied to your husband's behavior. You may unrealistically want your mate to be your ultimate source of personal stability. This invites the kind of friction we've been talking about because you become too coercive in your communication. Too pressing. Your mate may resort to his familiar evasive style partly because you're coming across as too emotionally overpowering or volatile.

As an interesting twist on this exercise, ask your husband to check this inventory as if he were you. His responses, assuming he's not fibbing in order to prevent some sort of blowup, might shed light on how you come across to him and others.

## Beginning the Journey Toward Improvement

If you are the mate of someone who scores high in noncommunication, realize that to some degree, the relational problems you've encountered are predictable. They show up in a lot of marriages. Also, there are some things of a general nature that you can do to ease them. For starters:

1. *Quit assuming responsibility for your spouse's imperfections.* He may well say, "You make me this way with your constant [nagging, whining, whatever]." That's not true, even though he may think it is. He would be acting the same way if he were married to someone else.

2. *Ease up on your persuasive efforts to convince your mate to fit your mold.* Coercion will only make the problem worse. This is hard to do when you desperately want change.

You've heard the stale old joke, "How many psychologists does it take to change a light bulb?

"Only one, but the light bulb has to want to change."

Down deep, you probably realize that no person is going to change, at least not effectively, based on someone else's forceful persuasion. An evasive husband will amend his ways only if given the room to do so in his own will. That leaves the ugly prospect that he will choose not to. We'll discuss that at length later. For now, it is wise to back off.

That does not mean that you quit doing anything.

"Good," said Ruth, "because I'm not the kind who can just sit back and do nothing."

One of my first suggestions to her was, "When you notice that Gary is behaving evasively, gently tell him you're feeling left out. By *gently* I mean without accusing him."

"I'm not sure I can. He makes me mad instantly when he ducks me like that."

"Okay, let's shift the picture a little. Let's say you have a close friend since grade school, a woman, and she's behaving in a damaging way. You see what's happening and, like you say, you can't just sit back. How would you tell her?"

Ruth mulled that a moment. "I see what you mean. Slip up alongside instead of slamming into her. I don't know. Treating Gary the way I'd treat a woman friend . . . That'll be hard. We've been at each other's throats for years."

"Very hard. You won't be 100 percent successful. It's not an easy turnaround. But the more you operate from the new position of friend, the more your situation may ease.

"Then second, show him some tolerance by letting him have the space he needs to absorb what you're saying."

"He doesn't hear it. It bounces right off him."

"Then so be it. Don't go overboard in making your point. And when you're looking for improvement, don't expect perfection instantly. Look for any little light in the forest. You're not giving up. You're shifting gears. The ways you've been pursuing didn't work. Time to try something else."

"That's for sure."

## What About You?

If you believe that your husband is ducking away from topics you are sure must be discussed, that he is becoming evasive in the midst of emotional exchanges, can you tell him about the frustration this creates without overworking the point or becoming confrontational? Everything will be working against you. The heat of the moment makes a person say things she would not say at a less emotional time. And most of all, old habits die hard. You are accustomed to addressing an issue in a particular way now. It is exceptionally hard to change your approach. But it will pay dividends if you can do it.

A word for husbands:

If your wife calls you evasive and accuses you of avoiding discussions she feels are necessary, are you open-minded enough to consider alternatives? When she says she's frustrated, that means she is frustrated, just as you may be. Something has to change.

Can you participate in the change with her? This teamwork is necessary if you are to move forward.

## Use What You Know

"I don't know much." Ruth seemed dubious.

"You've heard the term *codependency*?"

"Dysfunctional, right?"

"They're not synonymous, but that's close."

"I saw where someone said every family is dysfunctional some way."

I laughed. "In a sense it's true. The dysfunction I'm talking about, stated another way, would be, 'tactics that don't work and harm more than help.'"

To be dependent upon something means that your inner mood is controlled by that outer something or circumstances. *Co* means "together with." The term then implies that a system of dependency is in place involving both partners. You let your mood be controlled by me. I let mine be controlled by you. Neither of us is taking initiative because we are too busy reacting to the other, playing games of control and manipulation. In a nutshell, that is codependency.

Do you see yourself as having mutually dependent features? That's the question I asked Ruth and Gary, as I ask many couples. The situation is extremely common.

Gary wasn't buying it. "I've been called a lot of things, but nobody could call me dependent. I'm my own boss. I do my own thing. Very independent." He glanced at his wife as if to say, *And you aren't my boss either.*

"Ruth?"

"Independent. I'm on my own. I have to be, especially raising the kids. He sure doesn't provide any leadership."

I nodded; I expected these answers. "Gary? When Ruth asks you to do something, or tells you something, what's your automatic response?"

Gary might not have completed high school, but he was one

smart cookie. He saw where I was headed. It took him a moment, though, to shape his answer. "When Ruthie says something, I automatically think, 'no way,' right? So instead of thinking independently, I'm letting what she says make my choice for me." He sounded defeated in a sadly curious way.

"And Ruth? When Gary answers you, or fails to, how do you automatically feel?"

"Yeah, but I feel that way because I already know what he's going to say."

"Still, your frustration and anger are automatic, and they're immediately dependent on his responses. You two are certainly highly independent in your relationships with the rest of the world, which includes the children. But you depend on each other for the cues that govern responses and moods. You're both letting the other govern the way you respond and feel."

No one consciously determines to just let her mood or life choices be determined by the circumstances in front of her. For instance, you probably did not start today by saying, "Let's see. To whom will I hand my emotional stability?" Your dependency is far more subtle than that.

Each spouse enters marriage with certain ideas or expectations about how it should unfold. For instance, Gary started out expecting his wife to be friendly, supportive, and accommodating. Ruth expected Gary to be decisive, encouraging, and appreciative. These desires are both normal—in fact, unavoidable. But they are idealized. Not even Prince Charming is that perfect. Over time, probably not consciously, both realized that the other was not going to meet these expectations. Disillusionment brought disgruntlement, and their relationship began its slide.

Too, neither had a solid game plan for handling the unexpected emotions that accompany disillusionment. So, again, they slid into the dependency patterns we just looked at and assumed these emotions could be soothed by correcting the erring mate's behavior.

Like Gary and Ruth, you will need to know yourself well

enough to be aware of your potentially harmful patterns of emotional management. Personal soul-searching, as described in the following chapters, will help you turn things around and give positive traits to your marriage.

To get a good idea about how ready you are to do the soul-searching necessary for real growth, be aware of your use of one simple word. *You.* How often is that word spoken as you are trying to make sense of the tensions with your mate? I'm not suggesting that *you* should never be spoken. I *am* saying, though, that its overuse indicates that you are not looking inward.

In short, to improve your own satisfaction and happiness, a major step is to put your own house in order. You may find that the improvement in your life is just the catalyst your spouse needs. And even if you do not experience the adjustments in your mate that you have hoped for, you will still be a more stable and content individual.

Are you willing to start with your own hard, inward search?

The emotionally eager wife will say, "Yes! Of course." But then she amends that with a *but.* "I'm willing to adjust, *but* my husband needs to change." Whether or not you are correct to say this, there you are again, basing your happiness and responses on someone else's behavior.

In working with couples who are caught in the insistent-resistant pattern, I find there are three major trends that commonly surface on each side of the relationship. As each spouse persists with these patterns, they tend to make negative contributions to the marriage while simultaneously keeping the atmosphere fertile for the traits they like least in the partner.

As you read on, be willing to consider:

- His tendency to put performance first versus her tendency to put relationships first.
- His tendency to hide or bury emotions, particularly anger, versus her inclination to openly fret about frustrations.
- His reluctance to look at the insecurity that lies beneath his behavior versus her struggles with self-image.

Your willingness to buck these trends and either reduce or eliminate them will be the key for finding personal peace, then potentially, success in that most important relationship, your marriage.

*chapter 3*

# *H*is
# Performance
# Focus

Saturday mornings at the Sandstrom house tended to get off to a slow start, and they followed a set routine. Howard, the first one up, went through the elaborate process of brewing his coffee, viscous black liquid he referred to as his heart-starter. Fortifying himself with several cups of stuff that could chip a tooth, he parked at the kitchen table to absorb the newspaper. He started with the comics, went through the business section, then sports, then the front page. Local news, the crossword puzzle . . . everything followed a pattern.

Saturday mornings were quiet time, and he relished them. Such moments didn't happen often in his harried schedule.

Except this Saturday morning. Less than twenty minutes into his routine, Lynette came walking into the kitchen bleary-eyed, tying on her bathrobe. Lynette *always* slept at least another hour.

He waved toward the coffeemaker. "Still a cup left. You feeling all right?"

"Fine. Why?"

"You're up so early. Sleep okay?"

"Fine." She started the hot water running in the sink, poured herself a fourth of a cup of coffee, and diluted it to the brim with hot water. She scooped in a dollop of sugar. "It's gorgeous out today. I thought maybe we could just sit out on the deck and watch the sun come up and, you know, talk."

"Gee, Hon, that'd be great, but I want to be down at Hardware Heaven when they open. Get the gate hinges and toggle bolts. Lot of stuff I want to do today." Howard hopped to his feet and folded up the paper without even touching the crossword puzzle. "Here's the paper. Enjoy the deck view. You're right. It's gorgeous out."

"Howard . . . !"

He gave her a peck on the forehead. "Be back around ten."

Poof. He was gone.

Lynette sat fuming. The brush-off infuriated her. She'd even set her alarm to get up early when, presumably, he'd be more in a mood to talk awhile. Just a little while. She didn't expect the moon.

The longer she sat, the more tangled her thoughts became. Howard was a good husband in some respects. He was a steady worker who provided an excellent living. A good father to the boys, he never went out drinking with the guys. He wasn't a screamer, nor was he ever abusive. But when it came to simply talking to her, he was the pits.

"Why am I even married to him? He's always got something else to do," she complained to Kris later that day. "He can't sit still long enough to just share. Talk. Discuss personal things. He's either preoccupied about something at work or his head's in a ball game on TV. He'll sit for hours hacking at the computer. If he's not doing something, he's turned off. That's not a real husband! That's a major appliance."

Kris, her chin cupped in her hand, studied Lynette a moment. "I see your problem. Lack of communication." She held her hand out, palm up. "Five cents, please."

# 🌊 ASSESSING DEGREE OF FRUSTRATION

Can you relate to Lynette's frustration? Have you ever felt a pain stemming from the desire to have less busyness and more personal sharing? Do you feel that your man gives too much priority to tinkering and projects and not enough to the marriage? If so, you are not alone. One of the most common complaints I hear from wives is, "I wish I could make my husband slow down long enough to notice me."

Apart from coffee that can eat a hole in a tanker hull, would your husband relate comfortably to Howard—disappearing when any serious, in-depth conversation looms, feeling antsy or annoyed when cornered? When you try to share dreams and feelings or express needs, does he find ways to bypass the communication or sidetrack it onto something he's interested in?

As a very general rule, the male personality is less comfortable than the female when it comes to relating on a personal, intimate level. Please note, this is not a judgment. It's a description. The male personality is much more likely to talk about events—concrete things, such as the latest happenings at work—rather than unmeasurable intangibles, such as insecurities regarding his role as a parent.

In no way does this mean that men lack feelings. They experience the same range of emotions as do females, but they express them differently. And they certainly don't like exposing them.

Of course, this tendency of the male personality varies widely in individuals and is influenced by circumstances just as are female personalities. Ego blows and untoward events can make a fairly open man more reticent, and vice versa.

As a sort of rough-and-ready measure of how severely your husband suppresses feelings and tries to focus instead on tangibles and performance, check items below that often apply to you and your mate.

____ 1. When I talk about personal needs, he tends to call it nagging.

____ 2. When I tell him about my frustrations or dilemmas, I can't detect any significant sympathy. His response addresses only possible solutions. "Then why don't you try . . ." or "If I were you, I would . . ."

____ 3. At family get-togethers he has a hard time just sitting, catching up on one another. He wants to be watching TV or doing something somewhere.

____ 4. I've been complaining recently that we don't have enough one-on-one time.

____ 5. He does just fine carrying on a conversation about business or sports but not sensitive emotions.

____ 6. When our kids need help, he will talk to them about what they should be doing but not about how they are feeling.

____ 7. He doesn't seem to mind helping with household chores, but if I say, "We need to talk," he instantly loses interest in anything domestic.

____ 8. I can tell that he experiences a greater sense of accomplishment by finishing a project than after completing a heartfelt exchange.

____ 9. He thinks I let myself get too wrapped up in other people's problems.

____ 10. I have yet to hear him admit to major weakness or vulnerability.

____ 11. Any praise or encouragement he offers others is tied directly to an achievement.

____ 12. He has no idea how to respond if I start crying or express great frustration.

If you checked six or more items, your man probably possesses a strong tendency to place performance above relationships. Let me repeat that this is not a judgment. There is nothing wrong with being an achiever. After all, great satisfaction can be derived from jobs, chores, and activities—for men and women both. But the man so focused on doing and accomplishing can often step right over legitimate and necessary personal exchanges.

A part of any problem relates as well to the woman's degree of emphasis on relationships. A woman who is not particularly attuned to relationships would not find the problem with a man like Howard that Lynette did. But because Lynette was so strongly relationship-oriented, Howard's focus on performance particularly grated. In that area, in other words, they were mismatched. Both would have to adjust.

Fresh from her popover breakfast with Kris, Lynette was waiting for Howard when he returned with his hardware.

He bounded in the door as sunny as if nothing were amiss. "The boys upstairs?"

"Watching television. Howard!" She arrested him in his tracks. "Monday morning I'm making an appointment for joint counseling. If you value what little is left of our relationship, you'll be there." She walked out to weed the garden.

## GOING AGAINST THE GRAIN

A woman frustrated, as Lynette is, rarely stops to think how deeply entrenched her man's preference for performance is, or how he got that way. Girls are generally raised to value relationships and to work, as caregivers or peacemakers, to make them happy. The women those girls become assume that guys grew up similarly. Lynette, who grew up typically, did not realize that Howard was well-set in his ways long before he ever met the girl of his dreams. Both male and female manners of relating to others is virtually always a reflection of trained patterns from childhood. These are not whims of marriage; they are lifelong patterns.

To make a long story short, when next Lynette sat down in my office, Howard sat down beside her. Obviously, he was there against his better judgment. But he was there.

We began talking about the profound differences cited above. "Just for fun," I suggested, although of course the exercise was for enlightenment rather than fun, "each of you take this little quiz. It may point out your differences better than could a lecture." You try it also.

- During your teen years, to what degree was the value of achievement and a hard day's work emphasized?
- Were you very sports minded, focused on the thrill of victory?
- Did one or both of your parents take the time to discuss your feelings or personal philosophies with you, or were you just told, "Here's what you should be doing"?
- Was your father busy to the extent that it cut into the time he might have spent at leisure with you? How about your mother?
- To what degree were you made to feel that the favor of your parents and teachers hinged in large part upon academic success? Upon success in sports?
- To what degree were you expected to accommodate the idiosyncrasies of others and fit into a larger social pattern without making ripples, so to speak?

Now assume your husband took the above quiz. Would his answers differ significantly from yours? Better yet, if he'll do it, get the answers from him directly. Most people experience most of the above situations. It's the matter of degree—how much, how often—that differs so.

## Coming to Terms with Differences

There is nothing wrong, of course, with being competitive or committing to hard work. I have talked with numerous men who say, "You'd better believe I was an achiever in my earlier years. Still am. A growing boy needs to have strong encouragement to be his best. That's what I intend to convey to *my* children."

I then make the important point that I am not about to downplay the significance of being responsible. Instead, I emphasize that performance does not need to be taught to the exclusion of relationship skills. Both are equally important, and rarely are both taught to men in their formative years. This idea seemed revolutionary to Howard.

In one counseling session I gave him an assignment designed to assist him in becoming aware of his performance drive (assignments, acts of *doing*, cater to performance-oriented people). I asked him to inventory some of his typical, everyday exchanges with people he saw frequently. The assignment then was to write down what the actual communication was, whether it dealt with doing or feeling, and whether there might have been a relationship element he might have communicated. Here is a sampling of what he wrote:

■ **Tuesday**. My secretary had to leave for a couple of hours to take care of a sick child at school. I later forgot to ask her about the child's condition, but I was worried about how I was going to get some reports typed on time.

■ **Thursday night**. My younger son scored a goal in his soccer game, his first this season. We didn't mention how excited he was, but we did talk about some strategies that could help him score in their future games.

■ **Saturday**. Lynette had to work all day with a major volunteer project sponsored by the women's church league. We discussed some scheduling kinks, but I never thought to ask her how she felt about being a part of the project.

I might add that Lynette helped him write the list because on his own, he didn't see many of the opportunities to discuss feelings. Her comment: "I never realized." She had never grasped how strongly Howard was shaped to reject feelings and focus on performance.

The opposite is true also. It hardly ever occurs to men that women might have been shaped to value an attitude rarely expected from men.

As we discussed the list in our counseling session, I commented, "See how easy it is to give your attention to the doing aspects and how hard it is to notice the aspects of being? Of feelings? Believe me, I tend to be the same way myself. But Lynette—most women—are the opposite."

Howard admitted, "If Lynette hadn't pointed them out, I wouldn't have seen them. The personal aspects, I mean." He looked a bit sheepish and added, "And frankly, they're still not important to me. I tried to turn around the value I put on that kind of stuff, and I can't."

"Turn around a lifetime pattern in a couple of days? Of course not! Don't berate yourself that you can't. You were never taught that it has value. We're not working on assigning value to something now. We're working on seeing it. Finding it. Noticing it's there and recognizing that Lynette, with her different way of seeing, attaches great value to it."

Howard looked just plain relieved. "I thought you were going to try to turn me into one of those touchy-feely people."

"In a way, I am. I want to turn you into a person who realizes that there is a whole world of communication you're missing, to your loss. I can speak from personal experience. Thinking and communicating at this different level does not subtract the least bit from the pleasure you take now in performance and doing, and it adds a dimension that makes life much richer. And there's a highly desirable side effect: your marriage can be revitalized."

Lynette nodded sadly. "It's sure not very vital now."

If men are to expand beyond their present mind-set and reduce their evasive patterns, two major tendencies need to be reduced or even eliminated: 1) Allowing communication to be driven by competitive or performance considerations only, and 2) seeing emotions not as a natural part of being human but as a nuisance.

## Competitiveness Drives Communication

The goal of the achiever is superiority, getting ahead, being the best, and gaining control. Men experience a tremendous surge of energy as they sense they can accomplish a task better than the next guy. They enjoy feeling like the king of the hill, the conqueror, the go-to guy.

Is this quality wrong or harmful? No. *Someone* in a business or family or organization needs to be reliable. *Someone* needs to be the one who says: "You can count on me." It is normal for men to derive self-esteem from the ability to size up a situation and provide meaningful solutions. A day of achievement can allow him to go to bed at night thinking: "I got something done today. I matter."

Let me give you a very simple illustration from my home. Suppose I spend a Saturday sprucing up the yard. I plant seasonal flowers, trim the shrubs, weed the beds, trim the grass. Am I going to feel satisfied at the end of the day when I can step back and observe my handiwork? You bet! I performed specific tasks, major tasks whose fruits are easily seen, and I single-handedly made my yard look so appealing. With a positive sense of pride I relish the fact that I reached my goal of doing something concrete—of being useful.

I know men can relate to my feelings because when we get together we'll crow about our wonderful deeds! Men commonly like—I might even say need—projects that are physical rather than cerebral. Does all that give a man that inner feeling of necessity once he has achieved his goal? It sure does!

But let's take this thought one step further. As men function in the achievement mode, it influences their communication. Most men automatically adopt the competitive mind-set that is natural to them and slip into a style of talking or thinking in competitive terms. Again, the example of my day spent turning my yard into a thing of beauty. I wanted to know that someone noticed my superior achievement. I may have felt frustrated because I perceived that others did not pull their end of the load the way I thought they should. I could easily have become critical as I demanded that others maintain standards similar to mine. See how the competitive mind-set works? And none of this was going on at a conscious level, because at a conscious level, I was responding to training that I have to be nice and not boastful and not proud and not . . . You get the idea. In short, performance becomes the ultimate focus even when that's not what the man thinks he is thinking at all. Results, work, duty. These are the things he turns his attention toward as if they were all that mattered.

Regarding all my hard yard work. Am I going to be pleased if no one, especially my wife, notices what I have done? Absolutely not! Hey, I want her to praise me, to pat me on the back and tell me how I did a better job than the neighbor across the street. I want her to tell me she's nominating me for the "yard of the month" award.

Why? Why would I care if she notices? I think competitively. Like most men, I like to believe that my achievements separate me from the rest of the pack. My confidence has always been tied directly to my accomplishments. The icing on the cake comes when someone significant says: "Wow, you're the best!" I am capable of thinking that for myself, but that extra recognition can really keep me going.

Again I emphasize, at a conscious level the man may not be thinking these things at all. We're not talking about deliberate thought; we're talking about how the basic wiring has been laid out.

At first, Howard didn't quite get the idea about conscious thought versus the basic way men are programmed to approach life. "I'm like anyone else when it comes to being performance minded. I'll admit I get satisfaction when I see measurable results from my efforts, but I sure don't worry too much if people don't notice."

"Oh, give me a break!" Lynette glared at him. "How can you possibly sit there and say that? Don't you remember a couple of days ago when Gregg stopped in front of the house to show off his new car?" For my benefit she added, "Gregg's our neighbor three doors down. Gregg and Janie are about our age."

Howard looked blank. "So? He bought a Sunbird. Not a bad car."

"And as I recall, that was your comment exactly. 'Not a bad

car.' Fortunately, I think Gregg took that as an appreciative understatement. After he drove away, you went on and on about how he was no car expert, all the way into the house to the kitchen. Then you sat down and started in for the umpty-umpth time about that '68 Camaro you rebuilt with your very own hands and how *that* was what a great-looking car was supposed to look like."

"Okay." Howard still looked confused. "So maybe I did mention my old Camaro. What's your point?"

"You couldn't enjoy Gregg's new car because you needed to be recognized as one-up on him."

"Naaah!"

Yeah. That's competitiveness. See how Howard so automatically and unconsciously fell into the pattern? He never came close to realizing that, at an emotional level, his communications were determined by his drive to be just a little better than his friend. Lynette saw it only because she was so strongly oriented toward relationships. While he was thinking about and weighing automotive expertise, she was unconsciously analyzing and interpreting the interactions between the two men. As they talked in the kitchen later, she did not consciously realize the competitive nature of all this.

This foundational attitude does not surface only as competition. It colors and directs nearly every phase of a man's thoughts and communications. Let me offer some illustrations taken from counseling sessions (not just Gary and Ruth's or Howard and Lynette's).

■ Wife asks husband to be more sensitive and judicious in the way he admonishes their children. Husband replies, "Hey, you can be just as abrasive with them. Sometimes you're worse." He missed completely the real request—to weigh the infraction and respond more appropriately instead of coming down hard instantly and constantly. And that competition ogre raised its head as he compared his style against the harshest of hers.

■ A friend tells the husband about a bonus he received at work, and the husband complains to his wife, "Why does he get all the luck when I work twice as hard as he does?"

- The daughter tells the husband that she's learning her multiplication tables at school. She's quite proud. He responds, "When I was your age it was even more important to learn math because we didn't have calculators and computers like you do today."

- One evening, the wife asks about her husband's day, and he avoids discussing a major blunder he made because revealing imperfection makes him look bad.

I get this one constantly. In the male competitive mind-set, personal problems—even the hint of them—are serious imperfections because a competent, achieving male should be able to handle anything and make it right. Failure to do so, as evidenced by personal problems or errors of performance, diminishes the coveted "I'm best" status.

Women by and large have difficulty grasping this whole principle. Certainly, women are competitive. Fiercely so at times. But they've been trained subliminally from birth to be cooperative as well as competitive and to value some things in life along with or even above competition. They cannot easily appreciate a competition-first-last-and-always mind-set.

Can you see now how feelings of competition can push communication, particularly relationships between men and women, in a less-than-successful direction? I cannot overemphasize how important it is for a woman to realize that what she is interpreting as a personal attitude on the part of her husband (or any other male to whom she must relate closely, for that matter) is commonly unintentional and is a product of culture and masculine stereotypes.

## Personal Matters Are a Nuisance

A second major pattern of the performer is to minimize the importance of personal and emotional issues, automatically assuming that they are trivial and irrelevant to successful living.

Taking time to sift out human reactions is, by these persons, actually considered wasteful, since these matters can then detour from the more important goal of achievement.

Lynette sighed. "This is all a revelation to me. But you know? Finally understanding why Howard says what he says and does what he does and even understanding that it's not really personal with him—none of that makes the pain any less. It still hurts so much."

She then described an exchange that happened at the end of the last school year. After all this time, many months later, she still remembered it word for word.

She came home and excitedly announced, "I just learned that they're giving me a special plaque of commendation at the PTA end-of-year banquet. It's actually for continuing service, but mostly it's for my work putting together the silent auction. It's the first time in eight years they've awarded it. Mary told me about it an hour ago and I'm thrilled!"

"That's nice." Howard paused from waxing the Toyota. "Hey. Speaking of Mary, did she tell you anything about the boys' baseball round-robin this weekend?"

"Didn't you hear what I just said? Don't you remember all the phone calls and merchant contacts I had to make and all the hassle it took to put the auction together? Howard, someone noticed! They appreciate my efforts."

"I noticed the phone ringing a hundred times a day. Even Saturday mornings when we're supposed to have some peace and quiet. You might want to think twice about volunteering for that gig again next year."

"Howard Sandstrom, I'm trying to tell you some really good news, and I want you to feel excited with me, and you're worried about how much the phone rings!"

Now he was starting to act upset. "What are you getting all bent out of shape about? It was annoying, that's all. And I said it's nice. It's the first thing I said. You need a standing ovation or something?"

I will mercifully close the scene right there. Needless to say, it did not end at that point.

In our session, Howard agreed that Lynette's recitation of the incident was accurate. Then he added, "Until this minute right here, I never could figure out why she got so mad. I thought I was doing fine."

## Evading Emotion

On any given day, the average man encounters a variety of situations with a strong emotional element, affording that man the opportunity to explore and share emotionally. The average man will evade that opportunity in any of several ways. Let's set up some theoretical situations:

- His son tells him about a frustrating run-in with his social sciences teacher.
- His wife hangs up the phone. It is evident that she has been talking to a friend with a serious problem.
- A fellow employee starts talking about a stressful situation at home.
- His wife is upset because her day was extraordinarily hectic and she had no time to prepare the evening meal.

In each of these circumstances, a relationally oriented person such as Lynette would ask questions, drawing out the person. To the son she might say, "Oh, dear. Your Wednesdays are rough anyway, with band practice *and* phys ed. Tell me about it." An evasive response might be, "Well, you know what [the teacher] is like. Stay out of his way a couple days until you both cool off." The one sympathizes; the other immediately skips past any discussion of the situation and dives right into the solution, however impractical his solution may be (try staying out of the way of a teacher whose class you have every day).

The trick, for the evasive person of course, is to get away from the uncomfortable personal nature of the situation and onto more comfortable ground—doing instead of feeling. And don't forget the competitive aspect of this personality. The evasive person tends to achieve this in one of two ways:

- He provides a solution, as illustrated above, or
- He swaps story for story, often in a spirit of one-up.

The wife whose day was one big disaster from end to end might get, "You think your day was hectic. You should have seen what happened to me yesterday."

When a person places a high priority on performance or achievement, that person is going to feel most comfortable with the elements of life that can be neatly fit into slots. Black and white. Yes or no. That person wants to be able to measure the thing being considered, to understand it and in some way master it. There is an element of security to measuring and grasping.

Emotional responses cannot be measured, easily understood, or grasped. They remain their own wild things, never thoroughly controlled, certainly never easily evaluated. They never fit neatly into slots. They run the gamut of high and low, good and bad, in all degrees; and just when you think you might understand, they shift shape and nature. Emotions often defy logic and cut against the grain of the achievement mentality.

## Big Boys Don't Cry

On top of all that, our culture (as do most cultures) trains its males from infancy to be stoic with admonitions to be tough, don't cry, and never let them see you sweat.

Because of this training from earliest childhood onward, most males avoid grappling with deep personal issues. Even with peers, these people rarely feel comfortable exposing their innermost feelings. How much more important and necessary it was to maintain the proper exterior! Rare, indeed, were the boys who were encouraged or guided, let alone trained, to contemplate the directions they should take in relationships, to handle anger, and to deal with insecurities.

And so Gary Sweeney and Howard Sandstrom and multitudes

of other men sidestepped those issues and stayed focused on the things they could measure and things that counted for outside appearances.

## SEEKING THE ALTERNATIVE

Gary Sweeney sat in my office with his arms crossed. "I'm against it."

Ruth sat beside him. "I'll admit he's honest. When he says something, it's what he thinks. But almost all the time he doesn't say anything!"

Gary didn't give an inch. "This psychology stuff is a waste. It isn't how I operate. I'm a good worker, I've got a decent reputation, and I don't give my wife fits. So why—"

"Whaddaya mean, you don't give me fits? All the time!"

"I mean like running around or overspending or drinking. That kind of stuff."

"So as long as you're not an ax murderer, it's okay to rob convenience stores."

"Ruthie . . ." And Gary possessed enough native smarts to back off.

I chuckle to myself whenever I think about that exchange, mainly because I recall how inept I felt in trying to give Gary an explanation. And here's the reason explanations are inadequate:

He's right! He's absolutely right, *according to the values he grew up with.*

However! And it's a big, big *however.* "Not giving my wife fits" and "being a good husband" are not the same thing at all.

Students in agricultural schools and some vocational schools take courses in animal husbandry. They learn to nourish, nurture, propagate, care for, and improve the animals in their keep. The fruits of good husbandry are thriving, contented animals, not merely animals that must get along as best they can.

That's what husbandry means. That's what good husbandry is. Any farmer will tell you that on a farm that sings, the animals are in peak condition, producing at capacity because they are content and well cared for beyond the basics. It's just as true in the marriage between human husband of human wife. The wife of the wise husband is content and at her peak, whether the marriage be fairly new or fifty-plus years old.

Ruth and Lynette, not well husbanded, were frustrated to the point of distraction. Not nourished emotionally, not nurtured beyond the physical, certainly not encouraged. And yet, by their spouses' standards, they had nothing to complain about.

Do you see the dilemma?

So what must men do? Should they recognize the value of becoming less performance minded and more open to personal matters? Drop all their beloved projects? Completely restructure their personality and become wimps? Surrender the remote?

## Be a Man!

First, let's acknowledge that it is good—indeed, totally necessary—for men to act like men. Achievement, reliability, hard work. These things *need* to be maintained as part of a successful life. The trick is to step beyond that mind-set, to temper and enlarge it, and then to build upon it.

In counsel I urge men to consider the prospect that in a healthy marriage, they should not compete with their wives (the "You think your day was bad? You should have seen mine!" attitude). In fact, I encourage men to recognize that if they will, they can find ample satisfaction without being obsessed with competitiveness. I'm not talking about making the wife happier here. An excessive need to be the best can adversely affect your health. These are the guys with the increased risk of cardiovascular problems. And that's not to mention how their misery quotient goes up when, inevitably, the fellows fall short of their goals.

Lynette dipped her head toward Howard beside her. "You're talking to a pair of deaf ears here. He can't change."

Howard looked grim.

"Not change," I suggested. "Temper. Moderate. That is to say, think twice. I'm sure, Howard, you would agree to this: it takes a far stronger and more mature man to catch himself and adjust his relational behavior accordingly than a guy who pops off with whatever's easy to say. Anyone can speak without thinking about it."

I turned my attention to Lynette. "And I strongly recommend against you nagging or commenting at length unless it's a positive recognition of improvement. If he commits what you feel is a blatant relationship error, a simple comment to remind him is sufficient. And if it's not, that's his problem, not yours."

Howard still looked grim, but he was brightening. "Trust me. You can count on Lynette for acid understatement."

## Desperately Seeking Success

In counseling both men and women I put forward this principle: Success is ultimately determined by the richness found in your relationships.

Here's an illustration. A person who is the casual acquaintance of a casual acquaintance holds a prestigious position in his state's government. His name has been mentioned for a national office. He is legally married. His alcoholic wife, a partial invalid, lives in a gated assisted-living community in a different state. Is that man successful? I submit that he has failed miserably at the only really important task that was ever put before him—a task he promised before God to fulfill so long as they both shall live.

I then ask the person in counsel, and almost always it's the husband, "Is that what you truly want to be?"

Howard expressed to me privately that he didn't want to be a so-so husband to Lynette. In fact, he wanted to be an outstanding husband, and up until now had always thought he was.

See? There's that old competitive urge kicking in again, and a most useful thing it is.

Gary admitted an even more interesting behavior. At first, he irritated Ruth deliberately at times, "just to get her goat," as he phrased it. She bugged him, and he wanted to bug her back. The game lost its fun as acrimony mounted. Now he didn't know he was doing it and wished he wouldn't.

"Is that good husbandry?" I asked.

"I hear you. But I don't know how to turn it around."

Gary, too, wanted to be a much-better-than-average husband, the kind of man the other wives all envied. Ah, competition.

For him and others, I suggest simply that in addition to whatever other approach they take, they train themselves to think also of the relational aspect. The habit comes with time, as does any habit. As did Gary's habit of deliberately bugging Ruth sometimes. A couple of illustrations can show what I mean:

- The wife tells her husband about their son's bad grade on a test. His first impulse is to suggest ways to improve the next one. But he pauses long enough to think about what his wife has done or not done, keeping in mind that she's into relationships primarily. The second impulse, the considered one, also leads him to say, "After all the effort you made in helping him with his homework, that must have been discouraging."
- She says she got a call from an old friend, and he asks, not really interested in knowing, "So how is _____?" Then he pauses long enough to consider the relationship the two women have enjoyed for some years. "I'm glad she called. I know how much you mean to each other." You see, the wife in this incident certainly knew already how much the friend meant to her. It was the husband's acknowledgment that made him very special just then.
- She complains that the unremitting wind and rain today made her shopping chores difficult, especially when she tried to bring home the new traverse rod and blinds. The husband rejoins with, "I hope you bought a plastic tarp to wrap the parts that stuck out the window." Solutions, whether solicited or not. But then, "I'm sorry you had such a bad time. You know I admire the way you get the job done regardless." Relational. And so, nurturing. That's good husbandry!

How does a person not in counsel get her husband to see things in this new light? Corner him if you have to, but don't accuse. Explain that if he really wants to be a better-than-average husband, even say an adequate husband (as opposed to simply the guy married to you), he must try to notice how you feel. This of course applies in spades to relationships with the children. Children are extremely feeling creatures, and validating those feelings goes an enormous distance in helping them grow up emotionally healthy. Nurturing, nourishing, and caring are the hallmarks of good husbandry.

The goal is to learn how to recognize and acknowledge other humans, in particular the humans closest to the man, in their full dimension. The goal is achieved by attending to these personal considerations even as the man continues to pursue good performance competitively.

Wives can help immensely in this goal-setting and achievement, or they can hinder, even cancel, a husband's best efforts. In order to help a husband expand beyond performance orientation, the wife must also move closer to middle ground. The wife's feel-first focus is the subject of our next chapter.

## chapter 4

# *H*er Feel-First Focus

*B*ustling around in her kitchen, Ruth Sweeney poured more milk for Tiger, turned Gary's eggs (over easy, every morning), poked the bacon, and stuck four slices of bread in the toaster as she chatted on the telephone with her mother-in-law. The twenty-foot coiled cord between wall phone and receiver was stretched pretty much into a straight line.

"So then, his blade broke down again, and it put him two days behind. But apparently, he's finally getting caught up. It's been a rough couple of weeks."

His day still on remote control, Gary wandered in and filled his morning mug with Ruth's rocket-fuel coffee. His morning mug held two-and-a-half regular cups.

Ruth nodded to the person at the other end of the line. "Friday night's great. Is Frank coming?" Pause. "Good! G'bye, Mom." The cord dragged along the floor as she crossed the kitchen to hang the phone up.

Gary stood in the middle of the room, staring at her. "You didn't."

**59**

"Didn't what? Your eggs are ready." Ruth slid them onto a plate, added the bacon, and plucked two slices of toast as she passed the end counter.

Tiger yelled something about the bus, apparently addressing his sister upstairs from down in the kitchen, and ran out. His sister hollered from the staircase regarding a book report. The day had begun.

"Didn't set something up for Friday night." Gary flopped into his chair.

Ruth stopped in mid-bustle. "You have that look. Now what's the problem? You're not working early on Saturday again, are you?"

"These last two weeks have made joining a monastery look pretty good, and you want me to sparkle for my mommy on Friday night! Ruthie, what is it with you?!"

"Oh, come on, Gary! It's your mother. You haven't seen her in a month."

"And Frank."

"He's lonesome since his divorce. You can put up with your brother for a couple of hours." Ruth loaded her own plate and scooped up the other two slices of toast.

"No, I can't! I need a little hang time, Ruthie. Veg out. Unwind. Frank'll whine about his terrible life, and Mom will complain about her arthritis. I can't relax when I'm sitting there listening to that hooey. I've heard it all a hundred times already, the same old stuff over and over. I'm sick of it! And Frank hogs the remote."

Ruth poured herself a cup of coffee. "I wish you'd find some other record to play. That's what you say about any relatives I invite, and you complain about the friends we have in. I enjoy entertaining, Gary. Sitting here all day with your spreadsheets on my computer and three cranky kids underfoot gets old in a hurry. At least you get out and see people. I need people, too, you know." She sat down across from him and reached for the salt.

"But do you have to fill up the house with *those* people all the time? Can't you get someone who doesn't talk nonstop like an aluminum siding salesman?"

"They're your relatives. But then, nobody's quite the perfect guest, are they? I suppose you're the perfect host. I'm trying to be a good relative to your family because I like them. Is that so hard to understand? And you won't lift a finger to help with that. You sit there in front of the TV while I run around trying to make people feel comfortable."

Gary smirked. "Now you sound like Martha. You know, Mary and Martha when Jesus came to visit. Jesus praised Mary and told Martha she fiddled in the kitchen too much."

"I remind you, Mr. Bible Authority, that Mary was *not* sitting there watching *Wheel of Fortune!*"

## THE PROBLEM

When people are bound in the close intimacy of marriage, they learn to read each other. But this is not always the best thing. They also become locked into hearing what they think they're hearing and perceiving according to their own reckoning and not their mate's. When the wife responds emotionally, the husband figures there ought to be a logical basis for it. The wife assumes emotion and logic are two separate beasts. Each reads the other on his or her own terms.

Understand, I want to be careful to avoid stereotypes. Everyone knows women are not all driven by crazed emotions and men are not all merely intellectualizing machines. But as a rule, while women can be just as performance-oriented as men, they also tend to be more sensitive regarding emotional and relational matters. Notice I said "tend to." This can be either helpful or harmful depending on how that sensitivity is directed.

One thing is certain: Many husbands respond poorly to what women say and their manner of expression because the female style of communication is *so* different from male communication.

My long experience working with couples tells me that another factor enters the equation also. Let me illustrate with an exchange Gary described.

"I came in for lunch like usual, and Ruthie had sloppy joes ready. Everything was going great. Cheerful and upbeat. And frankly, I was feeling frisky, but of course that was going to have to wait because the guys were expecting me to get back to the site. So I made some sort of comments about buns. That the sloppy joes were on. You know, a double entendre."

"Nothing double about it," Ruth muttered.

Gary continued, "I guess she took something wrong, because when I came back an hour later to pick up some building permits, she blew up on me. Mad as a cat in a downpour."

Ruth stared at him. "You *guess*!" She looked at me. "Do you know what this jerk said?"

Undaunted, Gary pressed hastily on. "Then I said, 'Ruthie, is this your time of month?'" Gary nearly paled at the memory. "And then she *really* blew up."

Frequently, like Gary, men are baffled by a woman's emotional swings. Gary explained it to me this way. "Ruthie's emotions are like a giant exposed nerve, only you don't know where it is. Touch it by accident, and she orbits."

They assume that their wives are somehow so tied to emotional and relational cravings that they cannot see past the feelings of the moment. And very, very frequently, they also assume that a woman's emotional bungee cord is somehow controlled by menses.

There is a grain of truth to the part about menses. As their cycle progresses, some women, though not most by any means, experience wide swings in amounts of certain hormones. When their hormone levels are especially low just prior to menstruation, these women tend to have depressive and irritable behaviors. Negative things affect them more strongly, and they cry more easily. With the onset of menstruation, the estrogens begin to build again, and the world brightens. The phenomenon also occurs in some women entering their change of life and the cessation of monthly periods.

The great majority of women are not significantly governed by these factors. They resent intensely the suggestion that they are slaves to some primal urge and their men are the unwitting victims. Those women who are subject to mood fluctuations usually figure out what's happening fairly early on and allow for it. They, too, resent the implication that their behavior is governed by a mysterious ailment.

Worst of all, when a man thinks "time of month," he instantly discounts what the woman is saying. He assumes that she wouldn't be saying this during a quieter time, or at least she'd be more circumspect in her opinion. By attributing what he is seeing and hearing to a biological function, he need not take it seriously. This infuriates women, and why not?

Why, then, do men instantly think "time of month" when they get crosswise of a woman? For one reason, let's face it, it's an easy out. Don't bother trying to sort out complexities if a simplistic explanation sounds good. But the greater reason by far is the swift, casual way most women can shift mood. It really is not unusual or difficult for a woman to experience genuine joy, anger, sorrow, and boredom all in a few-hour period. The shifts are natural and spontaneous, not geared in any way to hormonal or other physiological factors. They are as much a part of her as performance and competition are a part of him.

This emotional volatility is foreign to most men. Although they certainly feel emotions as strongly as do women, they rarely shift emotions so quickly. If they're mad, they're mad. If they're happy, hey! Life's great! Because they usually do not experience quite the same volatility that some women do, they do not innately understand it, so they assign it to some physiological function they also do not understand and kiss it off.

Meanwhile, their women become further incensed because they are being discounted or even dismissed, and their attempts at communication spiral right down the drain.

To quote Ruth's comment to Gary, "Just because I'm not as stoic as you are doesn't mean my brain's out in the woodshed."

Lynette and Howard went round and round for exactly that reason. Howard could not grasp that Lynette's mood shifts might be natural and did not affect her insight. He assumed that if her emotional responses were extreme, her rational thinking must be blotted out. After all, if he got as mad as she did, he wouldn't be able to think straight.

Wrong. What's really happening here? She registers feelings that he considers illogical or exaggerated. Feelings that are extreme for the situation, sudden, and therefore unexpected. He retreats, deciding (probably below conscious level) that whatever response he makes will be drowned in the sea of emotion he's seeing. The more she tries to force him to give and take, the more her volume rises. The more he tunes her out, the stronger her emotions emerge. What might have been a discussion becomes a battle with only one certainty. No one is going to win the war.

As Lynette described it, "He clams up, and I keep getting more and more frustrated. I feel like a team of wild mules couldn't get him to open up and talk things out. But they're things that have to be talked about."

"Why should I open up?" he countered. "What good does it do when you're bouncing off the wall?"

"See? He makes no effort to understand or accommodate my feelings."

"I understand that you make all these mountains out of little old molehills."

## Working Past the Problem

Let's begin here by stating the obvious. Women and men do not think the same. That's no great revelation. Why even mention something so elementary?

Here's why. When husbands and wives begin the honest effort of opening their thoughts to each other, simple facts like this one are summarily dismissed.

In hindsight, outside the heat of battle, both partners can easily say that women process thoughts through a filter unlike a man's. And yet, as husband/wife discussions escalate, they automatically slip into the mode of thinking, "He should see things as I do." "She should reason like I do."

How do we turn that into a productive bit of information?

Wives, let's acknowledge that you can at times let your emotions lead. This is neither correct nor incorrect. It just is. Oftentimes it can be valuable, as emotions lead you to insight that would not be possible otherwise. But letting emotions have their way is not a mode of thinking that husbands can, by and large, comprehend.

Understanding this, I ask you to nonjudgmentally consider the prospect, "Does my husband retreat into his evasive patterns because he doesn't know what to do with my emotional style?"

As you recognize that this might be a possibility, you can then ask the question that leads to solutions. "How might I adjust my approach so as to minimize the problem?"

Today's woman instantly bristles at the thought. "Why should I have to be the one who changes my whole way of thinking just so he doesn't have to feel uncomfortable?"

Actually, that's not what I'm saying. You are certainly in no way responsible for restructuring your personality in order to keep your husband from exhibiting bad habits. But you *are* a team player. The two of you are supposed to be on the same side.

In the last chapter we recognized how wives can help men acknowledge their strong focus on performance and competition, substituting a goal of putting more effort into subjective elements and relationship matters. Now let us examine how a wife can be so feeling-oriented that her husband becomes bewildered and has no idea how to relate to her.

Just as men need not apologize for their focus on performance, so, too, women need not apologize for their focus on feelings. However, as men ought to move closer to middle ground and benefit thereby, women can too. They can contribute to their own personal stability if they can determine how to keep their emotions and emotional reactions from going too far to the extreme.

How strongly do you tend to lead with your feelings? It's an interesting and useful aspect of yourself to know. Check the following items that often apply to you:

_____ **1.** Feeling securely bonded to a family member or close friend is a very important priority to me.

_____ **2.** As I analyze the personal interactions in my relationships, I can see that perhaps I interpret conflict as rejection.

_____ **3.** I love to just talk and to feel close to people. I value intimacy beyond the usual "How's the weather" stuff.

_____ **4.** There have been times when I have wished my husband cared about relationship concerns as much as I do.

_____ **5.** I am generally far more inclined than my spouse to discuss the status of our relationship. I will initiate such discussions more often than he does.

_____ **6.** When disagreements arise, my emotional response to them can cause me to feel pessimistic or flustered.

_____ **7.** I have had difficulty being sexual because my mate seems to expect me to turn on even when we have had little closeness in the preceding hours or days.

_____ **8.** I sometimes reveal personal matters to close friends, knowing my husband would not feel as comfortable about that as I do.

_____ **9.** I appreciate being reminded that I am special. In fact, I need it.

_____ **10.** My husband tells me I remember details of past family interactions long after he has forgotten about them.

_____ **11.** Maybe I have overidealized what marriage should be, but that's honestly how I think.

_____ **12.** I feel as if it's my role and even my responsibility to keep family members pleased and upbeat. Someone has to.

A score of six or more indicates that your feelings play a strong role in your personal interactions. Good for you! Not only is this not bad, it indicates that you often bring out a healthy dimension of expressiveness in marital communication. You may be inclined toward major disappointment, though, if your husband does not score as strongly as you.

In fact, you will need to guard against the tendency to press your style onto him. He can never be expected to think like you. However, looking at life from your own relationship-oriented attitude instead of recognizing that others may not have the same attitude can produce some serious pitfalls.

## The "Does He Really Care?" Dilemma

One of the most serious of relationship pitfalls may be the concern that your spouse does not care nearly as much about you or about making the relationship work as you do.

Lynette had an excellent question in response to this. "Okay. I'm looking at our marriage differently than Howard does. But how can I tell if he really doesn't give a rip anymore or if it's just a difference in attitudes?"

So we explored the problem of insecurities for a while.

Lynette acknowledged the change in her marriage that comes in every marriage. "Howard was so attentive at first! But it didn't take long for him to become preoccupied by other things. His work. All right. I'd grant that. He was just getting established. Outdoor interests. That was no surprise. He's always been into sports. But television! I couldn't see any excuse for watching six straight hours of football. I began to wonder then if there was something wrong with me." She shrugged. "But then the boys were born and they kept my hands full being mommy."

At the end of one session, I left her with this to think about. "Think back to when your boys were born or before. Do you recall how your emotions then affected your communication style?"

She had to think about that one a good long while. The next week she came back with, "I fluctuated. Sometimes I'd hold my feelings in and try to be the sweet, loving wife. I was going to win him with sugar, you know? That approach worked just great to keep him coming around for sex, but I still didn't feel like he was interested in me personally. And certainly not my feelings."

"Has that approach changed?"

"A couple of times over. There was a period when I sulked. He'd get mad at me because he didn't see any reason why I should be unhappy. Then sometimes I'd get angry and let him know in no uncertain terms how disappointed I felt. And there were times I'd just retreat and cry."

"And his response?"

"He didn't respond appropriately to any of it, as far as I was concerned."

"How has it affected your marriage?"

"Negatively." She didn't have to think long about that one. "It depends on Howard's mood. If he's got things to do, he simply evades me. Stays out of the way. And when he can't do that, he walks on eggs around me. Tries to avoid anything about emotions so as not to set me off. Cautious." She looked ready for tears. "Obviously, both those responses are exactly the opposite of what I yearn for—emotional closeness.

"And admittedly, I have had yo-yo emotions. Sometimes I get so flustered I can't contain myself; sometimes I sink low and wonder 'What's the use?'"

Emotions should not be suppressed. They add variety and color to life. They make us feel alive, reminding us of the richness that can be found in the nonperformance elements of life. Without emotions we would not act protectively toward our kids, we would view a stunning sunset with apathy, we would have no reason to be encouraging or tender or loyal. The Creator ingeniously gave us emotions for the purpose of bringing fullness and contentment and connectedness into our lives.

But it is possible to have too much of a good thing. Left unchecked, our emotions can be an impetus for tremendous pain. While no one can choose to eliminate the presence of emotions, it is possible to develop mental safeguards so the emotions do not overplay their usefulness. In the case of a wife like Lynette, she needed to continue to feel what she felt *without* letting those experiences lead to disastrous communications.

Ruth Sweeney did not experience the feelings of insecurity that Lynette talked about. True, part of it was that her three kids came early in the marriage when she and Gary were struggling to build the business. Learning appropriate accounting procedures and computer skills, supporting Gary as he expanded his equipment inventory, and, to quote her, "keeping three healthy kids from drawing blood," gave her no time to think. But then, Ruth's emotional profile differs from Lynette's. Ruth is not as introspective. She frankly doesn't care as much if Gary is weak about discussing emotions. That's not as important to her. Parenting skills, socialization, the practical give-and-take of marriage, and help balancing her life are very important, and Gary was also evading those factors.

Ruth's and Lynette's attitudes toward emotional fulfillment differed greatly, mostly in degree. That contrast arose from the differences in the two women's basic personalities and, to a limited extent, their lifestyles. Ruth absolutely did *not* "think like a man." She thought like Ruth, and she knew what she needed and wanted. Lynette, too, knew what she needed.

It is possible to keep your emotions in balance by modifying two tendencies and holding them in check. They are: 1) letting your emotions define reality, and 2) reacting first, with little forethought to healthy alternatives and initiatives.

## Emotions Can Define Reality

Because emotional responses vary so widely from one person to the next, and from one event to the next, everyone acknowledges their erratic nature. You may feel excited about an event with which I am barely concerned. I may be amused by something you consider to be dull. Neither of us would be more accurate or appropriate in our feelings than the other. We are merely illustrating how unique we each can be.

Emotions can be difficult to fit into slots because no particular set of facts define them. No logic can sufficiently explain them. They lie outside the realm of measurable data. This is why you will often hear people explaining their emotions with phrases such as, "Something tells me . . ." or "I've got a gut feeling that . . ."

Some spouses, though, and we are focusing primarily on wives now, forget how greatly emotional reactions vary. They tend to respond to their mates as if their emotions and their mates' should be the same. Why? Because, forgetting how many reasons there are for emotional responses to vary, they fall into the pit of thinking, "If this particular thing feels this way to me, it should feel that way to you also." The wife's emotions have become a defining point for reality. Not, "This event feels this way to me," but "This event is this way." And that's dangerous.

Go back to the opening illustration in this chapter and recall Ruth's impatience when Gary resisted her efforts to schedule Friday night with relatives. What were the facts? Ruth enjoyed her mother-in-law's company and was happy to entertain her with dinner. She didn't mind Frank, for she understood in part the turmoil he was going through. She related more easily to the emotional aspect of Frank's circumstance than Gary did. Feeling that his time was valuable (which it was), Gary didn't want to spend it on activities—relating to his mother and brother—that not only were of scant interest to him but downright annoying. He needed off time when he didn't have to do anything. Having to "make nice" was doing something strenuous in his book. Neither person was immoral or weird in his or her thinking.

Now, take that scene a step further. How were the facts distorted? Ruth, emotionally attuned to both her mother-in-law and Frank and with those emotions leading the way, assumed that Gary was not interested in her outreach. She had social needs, and he ignored them as well. She felt that her efforts were rejected, and therefore she was rejected. That's a normal feeling. We all have it when rejection looms.

Admittedly, his communication was less than perfect, but was Gary rejecting her? No. Still, she was responding to him as if that were the hard reality. The conversation fell apart quickly (actually, it deteriorated to slam-bang; Ruth is very good at puncturing Gary) because she allowed herself to believe what her feelings were telling her. Gary responded poorly in large part because he was misread.

Have you found yourself letting an emotional response dictate the "reality" of a situation? Here are some instances I've gleaned from clients:

- A husband eats only part of his dinner, then retreats to the den, wearied by his stressful day, seeking some time to unwind and relax. His wife, however, wondering why he is so dissatisfied with her company, feels offended.
- The wife shares with her husband about their teenager's bad day at school. He replies, "I'll think about it." She interprets this as anger silently building, whereas he is not at all angry, just uncertain about how to handle the situation.
- As the wife plans leisure time with a close friend, her husband mentions how this will require him to rearrange his schedule to accommodate supervising their children during that time. He's not offended, he's just thinking out loud. She feels guilty, certain that he does not approve of her plans.

Every married person will admit (usually with a sheepish grin) how commonly husbands and wives can misread each other, no matter how long they've been married. Emotional responses can be so varied that they are always subject to misinterpretation.

The point is this: Emotions, whether they be experienced directly or interpreted in someone else, may have little to do with the overall truth of who we fully are. They are indicators (and at times unreliable indicators), of our needs and perceptions for the moment. They cannot be given the same status as hard truth since they are so subject to change or miscalculation.

Simple as the idea may seem, a wife can do herself and her

marriage a huge favor by keeping in mind the dissonance between emotion and reality. Sometimes an emotional response—a gut feeling—leads directly to a very accurate perception of another person. But just as easily, it may be far off base. Do you remember the advice you received as a child to count to ten before reacting in anger? Let's build on that idea by saying it would be wise not to draw conclusions in the midst of emotional exchanges until time is allowed and effort is made to decipher the facts of a situation.

## Reacting Before Initiating

When emotions are allowed to define reality, an unsettling pattern begins to develop. The wife too often becomes a reactor to events to such an extent that she fails to live according to her real beliefs or objectives. Instead of being an initiator who operates from a clear vision of who she wants to be, she is reduced to emotional expressions, behaviors, and communications that she does not like.

Ruth wrinkled her nose. "I don't get what you mean."

"Remember the pleasure and camaraderie you and Gary took in each other years ago?"

"I hadn't thought about that. It's true. We were more open with each other. More tolerant maybe. Less sniping. Not as cynical."

"Would you like the old days back?"

Silent pause. "Yeah."

"What's preventing it?"

In short, what keeps Ruth, Lynette, and you from being the kind of wife you intend to be? What hinders you from more closely approaching your ideal for marriage?

When I asked Lynette that question, her immediate response was, "Him. *He* keeps me off balance. I'm never quite sure of what to expect from him. He can be moody, and he's so inconsistent."

"Whoa!" Howard's eyes took on soccer ball proportions as he stared at her. "You're calling *me* moody and inconsistent! You, the one who invented bungee cords?"

I raised a hand. "Let's look at it inside out, so to speak. A new direction. Lynette, how does this sound? You presuppose an idea of how he ought to respond or feel in a particular situation. When his emotional response matches your expectations, you feel ordinary. The world is stable. When his responses do not—when he feels or responds in what you believe is an inappropriate way— then you feel unsettled, as if something is wrong. You could even say your own emotions turn sour."

She wrinkled her nose. "I see how that could be." She paused to mull the matter. "So you're saying that if he seems moody or inconsistent, then I automatically go into the dumps?"

"Well?" I paused. "Let's take as an example that incident when you learned you would be recognized by your service to the school group and Howard was cool to the news."

"That's putting it mildly."

"And you were humble, proud, and joyful."

"That's putting it mildly, too."

"Until you talked to Howard. You expected him to be as ebullient as you were. In fact, you thoroughly assumed he would be. And when he did not respond exactly as you anticipated . . . ?"

"I was devastated. I see."

"He wasn't deliberately out to spoil your moment; he just wasn't anywhere near the wavelength you were. Still, the bottom line is, you've essentially put him in charge of your inner direction."

Now her eyes were soccer ball size. "Oh, no!"

"It sounds like you're keying your own stability to your predictions of what his emotional responses should be. But they're unpredictable because emotions are not consistent. So when he behaves differently, you lose sight, at least for the moment, of what you want to be."

"That's terrifying! Howard is so . . ." Charitably, she let it slide.

I see it over and over. The woman considers herself Today's Woman, very much her own person. She certainly does not consciously choose to let her direction and emotions be determined by someone else. It slips up on her.

As I explained it to Lynette, "Sometimes a lack of initiative in this area can be very subtle. In the overall sense you may have a well-formulated goal of where you are going in your life. But in the emotion of the moment you are making split-second decisions based strictly on your reaction to him."

"More specifically, to my reactions to his reactions."

"Exactly. Real initiative is lost."

Are you aware of your unthinking reactions? Though you are not consciously intending it, you may in essence be saying to your mate, "Why don't I hand over my emotional stability to you? You can punch the buttons and tell me how I'm going to feel."

This tendency is risky, to say the least, given the fact that: 1) your husband is not a mind reader who knows exactly what you need each moment, and 2) even if he were, he is still very imperfect in his ability to make you feel on balance each moment you are together.

## Seeking the Alternative

Lynette asked precisely the right question. "How do I regain the initiative, the control of my own emotions?"

"You've fallen into this pattern over a long space of time. It will be hard to reverse it, but you can retrain yourself. For starters, let's pick two or three common scenarios when you are most susceptible to letting Howard control your mood."

"Easy," she replied. "Whenever I'm really enthusiastic about something. Also, when I'm feeling introspective or concerned. He turns into an ice cube, and it infuriates me. Saddens me too."

"Okay. Those will be good places to begin, then. Now I'm asking of you to picture in advance how you would choose to respond to those circumstances without letting your emotions be dictated by any outside source."

"Without losing control of them."

"Well put."

This is a ploy I commonly suggest to women who assume they cannot respond to their husbands with anything other than a strong emotional reaction, and usually a negative one. I know that in spite of the tendency to lead with emotions, women *can* take the initiative based on well-conceived choices. Taking the initiative requires that they will spend some time contemplating why they would select one response over another and get to know themselves better emotionally. It also requires them to choose emotional stability even when the spouse seems not to be playing fairly or appears callous and uncaring. This choosing is very difficult but not impossible. The women can then ultimately conclude that their emotions do not have to be dictated by the circumstances of the moment.

Let me underscore that the wife's objective is *not* the elimination of emotions. That's not going to happen, nor should it. Disallowing or stuffing natural feelings would be extremely injurious. She is not even trying to change them, really. She is regaining control. But even as she allows herself her full range of emotions, she can avert some potential problems by balancing them with some well-devised plans.

## The Balancing Act

First, ask the question: "How can I put my emotional nature to good use?"

Remember, it is your emotions that give you a dramatic flair, that prompt you to be keenly influenced by events, that draw out creative expressions. They are your essence, crystallized. And yet they seem to get in the way of smooth functioning in your marriage. Can this ever produce anything good?

Of course it can! You have something your spouse needs: pleasantness, spontaneity, joviality, tenderness—and yes, appropriate anger when you see a clear breach of the moral or ethical high ground. He needs to see all those emotions in action. And you are certainly doing him a favor by speaking about the subjective side of life.

Recently a husband (not Howard or Gary, though if they thought about it they'd agree) admitted to me that little delights at home tended to slip by without his attention. He explained, "My wife has a knack for discovering the things that are good in people. She's more tuned in. When our high school sophomore, Beth, came home with a blue ribbon on a science fair project, I simply commented on how proud I was of her work. It was a great project on anodizing aluminum. My wife, though, tuned in to the effort Beth put into it and how she felt. Not just felt about the blue ribbon but also about the process involved in putting the project together. It's amazing, my wife's ability to encourage Beth. She was so naturally tuned in to the inside of our daughter."

In the healthiest relationships, the man's performance focus is balanced by his wife's emotional focus, and each is tempered to enhance the other. Always I encourage the woman to learn to be unapologetic about her tendency toward emotional expressions as she recognizes the good it brings to the family atmosphere.

The opposite pertains, too, of course. Understanding that emotional expressions can be good, it is also true that a marriage can have too much of a good thing. Whereas many wives feel frustrated by their husbands' leaning toward the cut-and-dried logic, they can recognize that this logical inclination is not bad. These women need to be honest enough to admit that emotions, by their very personal nature, can invite a self-absorbed approach to life.

I have already mentioned that emotions sometimes operate with this false assumption: "If I feel this way, so should you." Of course, that is not a healthy approach to relationships, given the broad diversity of personalities and perceptions. So how about this for a second thought about the wife's emotional nature: Allow for the possibility that your perspective is not complete. It is always possible—in fact I would say it's highly· probably—that your emotions may be anchored in erroneous or partial data. Be big enough to admit that.

Let's go back to the opening incident in this chapter. Ruth made plans for Friday night that irked Gary. He didn't like having to spend his off time entertaining his mother and brother. She craved the social contact and sincerely wanted to build strong family relationships. Let's probe below the surface to see what was really going on here and how the situation might have been better.

Ruth could feel the negative emotional energy building. As soon as she saw Gary's very obvious "I-don't-like-this" expression, she went defensive. This emotional reaction led to an instant feeling of "here we go again," and the exchange spiraled downward.

Ruth's initial reaction, based not on her own feelings but on Gary's perceived attitude, might have been her cue to slow down and think. People need a cue to trigger changes in automatic responses. That would be hers. She might ask, in effect, "Am I building to a point where I'm losing control and letting reactive, automatic responses take over? Am I forfeiting the ability to reason?"

Another excellent question would be, "Are there other perspectives I need to consider? My mate's, for instance? Why are his feelings different?"

So let's replay the scenario as it might have been, had Ruth taken the initiative.

Ruth makes the arrangement for Friday night.

Gary protests, "You didn't" and explains why he doesn't want to do it.

Taking her cue, Ruth holds off on what she was ready to say (which is what she actually said). Instead: "This happens a lot, you notice? And when you pick it apart, it looks like your attitude toward your family and my attitude are poles apart."

She then could tap into a couple of different reservoirs. She might ask, "Why do you feel the way you do about your mom? About Frank?" Or she could take a different approach with, "How can we work a compromise here?" Sooner or later, the two of them are going to have to start looking at compromise. But notice, Gary's in a vulnerable position—just getting started with his day, and he's a slow starter. These are the times he's most likely to open up. What a lovely opportunity for Ruth to learn about Gary's deeper feelings!

Ruth might have learned that Gary's relationship with his mom has always been rife with friction because they are so different. Perhaps he and Frank have failed to deal with severe problems from the past that Ruth has never suspected. His complaints indicated something serious was going on below the surface, but Ruth's defensiveness and negativity blocked her from recognizing that something else might be going on. She attacked the surface when the problem actually lay far beneath.

That discussion then would open wide the door to compromise. Ruth backs off from pushing Gary into situations he so vividly dislikes, and he helps her toward the social and family contacts she wants.

Here are some other suggestions for women wanting to get past the present logjam of reaction and blinding emotion.

- Analyze recent incidents and devise a cue that warns you and tells you to stop and think.
- Don't get too wordy. I've found that many women feel that more words mean more attention (or any attention). Not so. In fact, it's usually the opposite. A few well-chosen words strike home better. So leave out minor details and if possible streamline the presentation. Stick to the point.
- Try to avoid overstating. "You *never* . . ." and "You *always* . . ." get the hearer thinking about exceptions to the statement rather than the statement itself. So much better to say something like, "You seem often to . . ."
- Don't repeat. Repeating a point indicates that the speaker is probably getting emotionally overcharged, and it invites an antagonistic response such as, "Oh come on! It's not all *that* bad!"
- Remember that you are trying to inform, not plead or persuade. If you would inform a man with a strong performance focus, you lay off the emotion and lean heavily to information.

The woman with a strong focus on emotions too often forgets that and falls back on her own preference rather than his.

## And When All Else Fails

Lynette wagged her head sadly. She sat in my office alone. Howard had other things to do. "Things are improving. Very much so. But I can't see that Howard is ever going to abandon his evasiveness. I can't believe he'll ever just sit down and talk about the things I want to talk about."

"Okay. He won't. Now what?"

She stared at me.

"We've been talking about reaction instead of initiative. Let's say he's going to slip into his old ways of disappearing out the door any time you want to talk. What initiative might you take?"

"Trip him?" It was good to see Lynette lightening up a little.

"How comprehensive is your medical insurance? What else?"

She thought a moment. "There's Kris."

"There is."

"But I want a high level of intimacy in my marriage as well."

"Marriage is the only acceptable venue for sexual intimacy. But sexual intimacy may not be 100 percent of both partners' hopes and expectation. If you need emotional and intellectual intimacy and stimulation, you may have to step beyond marriage. Within safe perimeters, of course—a trusted friend like Kris."

Emotional stability and satisfaction are important to every human being. If the wife hangs all her feelings out to her husband in the hope that he will somehow validate them without being told to do so, that woman is setting herself up for disappointment. She must enlist other allies, same-sex friends who can understand the parts of her that he may never understand. She, and you, cannot afford to hinge emotional stability entirely upon any one person's responses. People are simply too diverse.

A lot of this disappointment and negativity generates anger. So do other responses or lack of them. Let's look at the complexities of anger next, and how they may be influencing you.

**chapter 5**

# His Anger Imbalances

*K*eith Troy sat in front of me with the glazed look of a deer in the headlights. His was an emergency appointment. He was trying to make sense of the whirlwind he had been through in the past forty-eight hours.

"Okay, this is the picture so far. My wife and I had been arguing a couple of nights ago, and I got to the point where I just had to get away, so I got my car keys and left. I had to cool down, you know? She has a way of digging at me that just pushes all my buttons, and I couldn't afford to let it happen that night.

"About two hours later when I came home, the doors were bolted shut. Andrea had a note stuck under the front door knocker saying she'd had it with my anger, and she didn't have anything more to say to me. Here's the note right here." He dug in his back pocket. "So I've been in a motel the last two nights, you know? She won't let me back in the house."

"No communication at all?"

"I asked her to give me some clean underwear as, you know, a foot in the door? She dropped them out the upstairs window. I'll

**80**

tell you how determined she is. We have the kind of storm window system that she had to rip a screen out to do it."

"I'm assuming this is not the result of a simple onetime flare-up. Would it be safe to say she's been building toward this for quite some time?"

"Yeah, that's a pretty safe assumption. But I never guessed *all* this! You know? Hey, look. I'm not a rageaholic, at least I don't think I am. But Andrea has said a hundred times that she can't handle me when I start feeling ticked off. What's to handle? That's not her job. Anyway, she says I become irrational and shut her out. Believe me; lots of times I try to hold in my anger, but I guess it registers anyway, you know? She's said a couple of times recently that she's at her wits end with me. I don't know what to do, but we gotta do something." He looked distraught. "You know?"

I know.

## WALL OF ANGER

Anger can block communication even quicker than can Howard's or Gary's distance, and it contributes greatly to distancing. Moreover, it's dangerous. When laughter gets out of hand, no one gets hurt, emotionally or physically. Anger is a different matter.

One thing can be said with certainty about people, but especially about men: they can be incredibly inconsistent in the way they handle anger. One moment they hold it in, allowing it to develop roots of resentment, bitterness, and depression. Sometimes they'll let it uncork as explosions, leaving wives wondering, "Where in the world did that come from?" And don't they love to let it sneak out through sarcasm or biting comments or plain old edginess. And yet, at times when others would assume these folks should be irate, they remain totally calm.

Have I described your man? Don't be alarmed. He has plenty of company in this category. Most men display these characteristics to some extent—in fact, so do many women—but some go to unfortunate extremes. I am addressing the issue as it pertains to men in this chapter not because I'm saying they're the only ones who get angry, but because it is much more often the man's anger that disrupts family unity. A woman's anger takes somewhat different forms and usually produces different results as regards communication. So rest assured, I'm not suggesting that women's anger needs no attention. I am dealing with the impact men's anger has on the subject at hand—evasiveness and distancing.

Evasive and distant husbands often avoid close interactions because of unresolved anger. When a husband mishandles this emotion, the potential for marital camaraderie diminishes significantly. That makes the need for a solid game plan regarding anger management enormous. In short, men's capacity for closeness will be tied directly to their ability to change erratic anger patterns. And while it would be desirable if he would dig right in to try to reduce or dispose of those patterns, that rarely happens spontaneously. You needn't wait for him to step up to the plate. Learn all you can about his anger. It will help you reduce your own frustration, if nothing else. You'll be able to manage your response to him far more effectively than you can now.

Let's begin this chapter with a simple, thought-provoking question: Have you and your husband ever talked about his anger? More important, has either of you deeply contemplated the meaning of this anger? I know that people in my profession can seem eggheaded as we try to chase down answers to questions like this, but bear with me. Let's get theoretical for a moment. Before you know how to handle your anger you need to know what lies beneath it.

Keith and I talked at length about his history of tension with Andrea. The profile he presented sounded fairly innocent. It also sounded very familiar, for I hear so many stories similar to his.

From a decent family background, Keith's parents played traditional roles, dad away on the job and mother tending house. There wasn't much sharing on a deep, personal level, yet it was pleasant enough. As a young man he set out to make his mark in his profession, and he did that reasonably well. He and Andrea were brought together on a blind date. (Do you realize how many marriages come of blind dates?) That warm newlywed glow cooled in the struggle to establish themselves financially and raise the kids. As time passed, they grew increasingly wearied by each other's imperfections, which each could recite in a litany of woe. Friction began as irritations and spats and escalated as time passed. He considered her way too judgmental, critical, and nitpicky. She called him stubborn and prone to unjustified anger.

Over the years, Keith developed a wide repertoire of expressions of anger and tended to use them erratically. As he put it, he was unable to hold it in (that is, quell anger) while trying to cater to Andrea's numerous requests. At times he might shout, throwing in a few curse words, or perhaps pout and fume. He might explode wildly and a short time later act cool, as if nothing at all mattered to him.

Without admitting it to himself, Keith was letting anger set up residence within. He would not have phrased it as I am phrasing it here, but in essence, he had made a private commitment to let anger have a permanent hold on him. In the meantime, Andrea perceived him as being increasingly hard to reach.

## The Root Causes of Anger

What causes men like Keith to give themselves over to this gripping emotion of anger? To answer that, let's begin with a working definition of anger. Everyone realizes that this emotion *does not* arise because of perceptions of cooperation, friendliness, and encouragement. Anger arises when persons perceive the opposite: rejection, invalidation, coercion, misunderstanding, and being ignored. Also, anger does not have to be accompanied with shouting or viciousness, as some have assumed, to be called anger. It can be demonstrated in quiet frustration, impatience, annoyance, irritability, and responses termed "uptight."

Keith acknowledged that his yelling and swearing and throwing things ("I heaved a lamp against the wall, you know? That really freaked Andrea") were expressions of anger. "But not pouting, for Pete's sake. Everybody pouts. Everybody looks glum once in awhile. That's all it is. Feeling glum."

It's anger.

If you dig down to the very core of anger, you find fear, but not the fear we think of as fear. This is a primal fear, a person's perceived need for self-preservation. Specifically, the angry person is wishing to preserve:

- Personal worth and ego ("Hey, you need to treat me with respect.")
- Personal needs, which include personal safety and understanding ("Can't you recognize that I have needs like everyone else?")
- Strong convictions ("I have my beliefs, and I'm not going to back down from them.")

Keith possessed all of these in his relationship with Andrea. It caused him to be fully convinced that Andrea had ceased to really care about him as a person.

"She's always talking down to me," he complained (personal worth questioned). "Especially with her infernal honey-do list. Except she doesn't even say the 'honey' anymore, you know? I get home from work and it's 'Do this, do that.' Once she even told me where the ice cubes were!" (lack of respect for intelligence, an ego-deflator). "Can't she see that I've got to have some understanding when I get home?" (needs unmet). "I don't care how right she thinks she is, I'm not going to let her or anyone else tell me how to live" (holding strong convictions).

Is it wrong for a person to register anger and let it guide communication? Certainly not at times. Were this a perfect world, there would be no requirement for anger; for worth, needs, and convictions would be harmoniously upheld by others. But because this old world is so horribly imperfect, others respond in ways that bring disharmony and conflict, either intentionally or unintentionally. Managed well, anger can become the springboard that prompts persons to address conflicts with the intent of creating a more constructive style of relating.

But as is so often the case, what potentially can be put to constructive use can be misappropriated, often with disastrous results.

## Identifying the Extent of the Problem

Keith did not recognize the extent of his fire inside. Andrea did, more with intuition than head knowledge, but she could not articulate it. It's hard to identify sometimes, let alone quantify. Here's a little quiz that may help in that task. Remember that everyone experiences anger. There is no question of whether it's present. The question is whether that anger crosses the line from appropriate to inappropriate. Again, we're assuming that the spouse harboring unhealthy anger is the male. Check the items that sometimes apply.

_____ 1. When my husband states a belief or strong conviction, his words take on so sharp an edge that I am offended or frightened.

_____ 2. At times, I perceive that my husband does not have constructive intentions when we are in conflict. That is, he's not trying to correct or ease the situation and may even be exacerbating it.

_____ 3. He's often grouchy.

_____ 4. I and others in our families call him stubborn or hard-headed.

_____ 5. In my opinion, impatience is too much a part of his personality.

_____ 6. He'll stew or brood over problems for hours at a time. He has a hard time letting go of a problem or source of anger.

_____ 7. Heaven forbid I snap at him; he snaps right back.

_____ 8 He doesn't take criticism well at all. Not in any form.

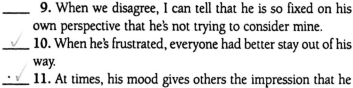

_____ 9. When we disagree, I can tell that he is so fixed on his own perspective that he's not trying to consider mine.

✓ 10. When he's frustrated, everyone had better stay out of his way.

✓ 11. At times, his mood gives others the impression that he is indifferent or unconcerned.

_____ 12. When he's disagreeing with someone he'll hammer on the same point over and over again.

It is no crime to admit that neither you nor your husband always handle your anger perfectly, but a lot of men feel it is. Frankly, the man isn't about to see a need for change until he can feel more open about flaws (there's that performance/competition factor again). If you checked six or more items, some major adjustments are probably in order. This person needs help learning to better handle anger. Let's examine some key issues that could make a real difference.

As Keith and I talked, one of my comments was, "You've been describing some pretty nasty episodes. It's good that you're not denying your anger."

"What's to deny? When we really get into it, Andrea and I, it's right out there for everyone to see, you know? But I deny it's the problem she seems to think it is."

"If she perceives it as a problem, then it's a problem for her. Since you're her husband, if you can solve it for her, it's worth it to you to think about resolving it. Has it ever seemed a problem to others?"

"My mom lately, but she's always been down on me. I got fired last year for getting mad, but that was justified anger, you know? If that dolt treated you the way he treated me, you'd have been fired too."

"All the same, anger causes problems beyond your marriage now and then."

"Yeah. But, you know."

Extenuating circumstances. We bandied that about a few minutes more and finally got to the bottom line. He harbored persistent anger, regardless of the cause. We went on to the next big decision a man submerged in anger must make.

"Keith, you came in here agreeing that you had to do something about your situation with your wife. Here's a major step forward for you to make. Decide and agree that this will not be allowed to continue as it always has."

It's one thing to say, "I get angry from time to time." It's an entirely different matter to say, "This is an ongoing problem that will no longer be tolerated."

I wish Keith had said, "Yeah, I need to get a grip on it no matter how hard it will be. Andrea has lost a lot of confidence in me, and it's going to take a major turnaround on my part to regain her trust. But whatever it takes, I've got to get to the bottom of this problem." With that kind of commitment, working with him would be a highly productive piece of cake.

He didn't. But he did agree that he needed help with a problem that was not resolving itself and committed to a series of sessions to work on it.

In order to help these men drop their evasive guards, I get them to examine the underlying causes for their anger. We look at such issues as their need for respect, their craving for control, and their history of unresolved hurt and grief. You the wife are not a counselor as such, but you are, if typical, well attuned to your man. Let me show you how we approach the three root problems in counsel, so that you know the process.

## The Cry for Respect

If anger represents anything, it can foremost be understood as crying out to be respected. The implication is that the angry person feels he is not being given due consideration. Angry husbands, like Keith, have convinced themselves that others hold too low a regard for them. Whether their perception is accurate or not is largely immaterial. They are reacting to the perception. Their anger is a response, their communication of it an attempt, usually not a conscious move, to remedy the slight. Regardless of whether the anger is accompanied by loud shouting or by quiet and stubborn withdrawal, it is pushed along by the thought, often below conscious level, "No one is supposed to treat *me* like a lowly nothing."

Here are some situations I've come across more than once. Notice how they show the link between anger and the craving for respect:

- As the husband is explaining his reason for approaching a particular task in a particular way (let's use managing the budget as an example), his wife interjects with alternative suggestions. He becomes instantly angry. His verbalized reason: "You know how I hate being interrupted!" But on a deeper level, he sees her as invalidating his logic.
- A perfectionist husband fumes because of the mess lying around his house. On the surface he can say he is ticked off because of clutter, but really he is feeling, "I've declared my expectation for order a hundred times, but no one takes me seriously."
- At the end of the day, the husband is agitated because his wife is yelling at the kids and the kids are yelling at each other—in short, being normal kids. He roars aloud his desire for a little peace and harmony. Down inside, though: "Doesn't anyone understand that I don't need to come home to face this garbage? When are you people going to respect *my preferences?*"

Each of these episodes of anger is pushed by the human desire to be accorded thoughtfulness and consideration. Let's even say deference. Deference is a sure sign of respect. Even the seemingly thick-skinned man hungers to know that his worth is acknowledged by others by their open display of sensitivity to his needs and preferences.

I said to Keith, "Let me put forward this idea for you to think about. One big reason you struggle with anger is that you powerfully crave your wife's respect. Of all the people in a man's life that he wants to stand tall before, the woman he won is first."

Keith was not accustomed to thinking about such matters. His first response: "I don't need anything from her." He admitted, though, "I get so tired of Andrea putting me down, you know?" The idea had taken root. We went on.

I could safely assume that his Andrea was not the first person in his life to show what he considered disrespect, so I asked, "What other people have disappointed you by not showing you the full respect you feel you deserve?"

That opened a floodgate. He never managed to win his parents' approval, and particularly that of his father. "I was always having to figure out how to stay on his good side." As we talked, Keith recognized that his father also harbored a lot of anger. In fact, Keith could identify the signs in his father much better than he could see them in himself. That, though, was the door that led to him discovering his own burning inner fury. He went on to discuss at length how through the years he felt a hole inside because he was not given the respect he thought was due him by many other people.

The anger that men like Keith feel shows just how hungry they can be for affirmation. Whether or not they put it in words, they are wishing for people to operate on the basic assumption that they have a God-given worth that should not be ignored or denied. But because they had virtually no training to identify such underlying meanings in their anger, they did not learn to communicate their convictions constructively. As a result, the anger emerges in ugly, abrasive ways that prohibit anyone from truly understanding or caring about the real issues that underlie it.

## The Craving for Control

Not only is anger a cry for respect, it also represents a desire for control.

Control is power. Power validates. Possession of power and

control brings with it respect. See the larger picture? Here's how it works.

As angry men sense that they are receiving foul treatment or are being threatened with it in some way, they assume (usually below conscious level) that they can remedy their problem by controlling others' opinions or attitudes or feelings. Too, control indicates that you're the top dog. Here's the performance-and-competition factor in still another form.

This desire for control can be evidenced in heavy-handed thoughts like "She's going to have to . . ." or "I've got to get her to . . ." or "Nobody is going to . . ." Angry men have bought into the false assumption that the way to find peace is to forcefully push their agenda on those who dissent. Come to think of it, whole nations and religious organizations fall into the same trap. Of course, this backfires since others with their own need for control do not want to come under anyone else's yoke.

Keith disagreed. "Andrea's kind of wishy-washy, you know? She doesn't have any craving for control, as you put it."

"Locking you out strikes me as a fairly extreme control measure for a wishy-washy person."

"Yes, but . . ." His brow puckered as he paused. "Yeah!"

Instead of seeing control tactics for what they are—fruitless—most angry men add to their frustration by pressing even harder. Fed by mistrust, anger implies, "I've got to be in charge of the way others see me or think about my ideas. I'm not taking any chance that I might be stepped on or manipulated."

When obvious control tactics are used, it is hard for angry men to deny the problem this creates. Some of these tactics include bossiness, threats, intimidation, punishment, and stubbornness. But when control is applied by more subtle means, these men may not be as willing to admit the problems they are creating with their controlling behavior. In other words, subtle control allows people to deny its very existence. Examples of subtle control are: not talking, sulking, promising to do something then not doing it, laziness (which is actually obstructionism—passive resistance), and refusal to admit faults. You'll recall, Gary Sweeney made a cottage industry out of controlling Ruth and the kids by these means. Who would call his behavior "control," let alone "anger"?

I wanted Keith (and Andrea as well) to understand how he was undermining his marriage by letting control cravings push his anger. "Some of your reasons for anger are normal," I explained, "but your anger is going too far when you assume that you can coerce your wife and others to respond as you want. Coercion doesn't work, and that makes you angrier. I suggest tnat your anger is perpetuated by the assumption that the conflicts in your life will cease if you can force agreement."

"Okay, I see your point. But a man's got a right to coerce his wife and children. He's the leader."

"Leadership and coercion are not the same at all. Any bully can attempt coercion. Besides, real leaders lead by example as well as authority."

I tried to impress upon Keith, as I counsel all control-driven men, that control is an illusion. "No matter how hard you try to control others, you won't succeed. She is protecting her own identity.

"Now think about what you would have if somehow you actually *could* control your wife. She'd cease being an equal. She was not created as a helpmate to be reduced to a robot or machine. I don't think that's what you really want."

For husbands to be approachable rather than evasive, they need to manage their emotions, with reality and harmony leading the way. Control tactics are neither realistic nor do they produce harmony. So in order to get desirable results, some thought adjustment is in order.

When I talk with men like Keith I often ask, "Would you be willing to free your wife to be whatever she chooses to be?" I am referring to more than just allowing freedom in physical matters, such as how she adjusts her schedule or how she spends money. Rather, I mean freedom in her attitudes, in her feelings, in her perceptions and needs. "Are you ready to admit that she's a fully functional adult and be willing to trust that she can manage her life reasonably?"

You would be surprised how many men cannot believe that an independent, freely functioning wife could possibly give the husband's needs priority.

The theory in releasing control is this: Each person acknowledges the other's freedom to be whatever he or she chooses to be and to believe. This certainly doesn't mean either would cease communicating needs, convictions, and preferences. Obviously, that would greatly perpetuate and exacerbate the pattern of evasiveness we're wanting to avoid. Rather, each is honest about who he or she is and what he or she believes. Both parties, however, express mutual respect and refrain from cutting down the other's sense of self (the technical phrasing would be invalidating his or her needs). Each party lets the other choose how to respond.

Do you see how this release of control would alter Lynette's attitude toward what she considered as callousness and distance on Howard's part? She would train and remind herself that he, being his own person, was free to respond naturally. And you're probably way ahead of me on this: Released from her unrealistic expectations, he would no longer possess that innate need to rebel, would not have to go to the opposite extreme as so many acts of rebellion do. By both moving more to the middle, no longer in a struggle for control, both would enjoy far greater harmony.

This applies to Keith and Andrea too. I pointed out to them, "Keith, you come down hard in a controlling way. Andrea, you counter that control attempt by, as he puts it, getting nitpicky. Your reaction is based on a feeling that it is somehow your job to make him stop the controlling behavior. And I repeat that very little of this is going on at a conscious level, where you can see it and root it out. In essence, you're making your own attempt to control. This increases his anger, which increases yours . . . see the cycle?"

"Fine." Andrea didn't act as though she thought it was fine at all. "Which one of us is supposed to back off and break the cycle?"

"Both. By all means."

Keith really struggled with letting go of control even though he agreed with the theory. For one thing, he found it difficult to admit how often he acted controlling at those times when his tactics were not of the overbearing variety. He also displayed his controlling anger through blank stares, quiet noncooperation, and rebuttals in communication. So his first task was to be honest regarding the ways his control played out.

But even more difficult for him was the idea of being tolerant and truly accepting when giving Andrea the space to react to him on her own terms. This meant being less opinionated in the delivery of his thoughts and being more open-minded regarding the legitimacy of her feelings and perceptions. For Keith, as for so many men whose anger is ingrained, it took him a long time to learn that healthy relationships employ a deliberate blend of straightforward communication and an acceptance of both partners' uniqueness. It was even harder to put that knowledge into action.

Andrea was not to expect miracles overnight. But her man was committed, and the change would come.

## Unresolved Grief and Pain

Anger does not arise from a vacuum. It may be set off by a current aggravating circumstance, but it also tends to be influenced by historical experiences of tension.

Keith grumbled, "It's not necessary for me to dig up historical traumas in order to understand the way I am now." You should have heard the sneer in his voice when he said *trauma*. I hear that so many times. While I am not the kind of counselor who pitches a tent and camps out in others' pasts, I do believe it is valid to acknowledge that much of current behavior is shaped by experiences in the formative years. That's when many adult habits and attitudes are formed.

When I begin the discovery of an evasive husband's anger, I almost always learn that pain from the past has not been appropriately grieved. Obvious sources include parents' divorce, death, and other severe loss. But it may also have been disappointment stemming from a mother's lack of nurturing, insecurity resulting from a father's harshness, loss of self-esteem related to less-than-perfect performance. Whatever it was, these men almost universally recall that their pain was not openly resolved or even deemed legitimate.

For instance, Keith mentioned at that first appointment how he struggled with his father's heavy-handedness in his early years. Later he elaborated. "My dad was pushy and impossible to please. No matter what I did, I could count on him carping about how I could have done better. But what's to grieve? That's just the way he was."

"Regardless, I'm sure that bothered you. It would bother any kid. Did you ever tell him how you just wanted to feel special to him?"

"Are you kidding? Dad? It would never occur to him to ask, and it never occurred to me to volunteer it. He didn't care about that kind of stuff, you know?"

Notice that last thought; he learned he could never expect his father's understanding. That's sad, and it is also reason to feel pain. So what did Keith do with his pain? "I wouldn't let it bother me, and I'd go on minding my own business."

I'm told that constantly, and I don't believe it for a minute. On the surface, yes, he continued with his responsibilities, but what about that statement, "I wouldn't let it bother me"? Of course it bothered him when his father was harsh! When his wife similarly treated him with disregard, he would register his anger in some fashion, but commonly his anger was stronger than the circumstance warranted. He was letting her feel the retaliation for whatever she had done to cause him pain *and* for the pain that had been stored inwardly for years.

## ◀ *INITIATING A CHANGE*

All these sources of anger are the man's problem. What can his wife do about it? Quite a bit.

For both spouses' sakes, the first thing is understanding. A mere, "Now, now, Dear, it's all right" pat on the head won't do. Real understanding. That will help the wife cope with his behavior and initiate her response rather than reacting automatically.

Try selling that to Andrea Troy. In a reversal of the common pattern in situations like these, Keith had a terrible time getting his wife to join in counseling. Wearied by the battle so long and hopelessly fought, she wanted nothing more to do with the whole thing. "That's his problem. When he solves it, we'll talk. Maybe." Maybe not. She was no longer certain she wanted to bother to save her relationship.

Keith begged. He wheedled. He made promises. He asked me to write a note assuring Andrea of his desire to do something. Only after he had demonstrated his new determination by attending four sessions by himself did she relent enough to come in and try one. Even then he had to drag her in kicking and screaming, figuratively speaking.

What I tried to convey to Andrea, let me also convey to you. The first order of business was to understand what was going on. The second was then to work from the wife's position seeking change. Andrea was fortunate that Keith wanted to change. Your husband may not. That doesn't mean in the least that you are a helpless victim. You can still act instead of react.

Can you lead your husband to understand some of these dynamics that have taken over his behavior? I don't know. Perhaps you can find opportunity or create it. Let me show how it works in counsel. You then can use the knowledge in whatever way seems to present itself. At the very least, you'll have a firmer grasp of what is going on and how to break the logjam that now hinders the flow of love.

To deal with the three major sources of anger, I may draw out insight by asking the person, Keith, for example, to consider a series of points. I then might challenge him in specific ways to make beneficial changes. Lastly I can suggest some practical ways to do that. We then discuss and deal with the anger itself.

Let's follow that pattern here, looking first to ease the sources.

## Reducing the Sources

*1. Respect.* First, recognize that whatever else it may stem from, your man's anger represents a deep hunger to be respected. And I'm sure you don't need me to tell you that his abrasive style of communicating anger will virtually guarantee that he will *not* receive the very respect he so desperately seeks. Be aware also that his strongly expressed anger implies a high degree of insecurity.

I ask the man, "Do you absolutely have to have the respect from others as desperately as your anger indicates that you do? How much is actual, driven need, and how much is simply conditioned expectations?"

I believe that a rewarding life is largely determined by our success in making personal connections, so yes, it is normal to crave respect. However, I present the counselee with this challenge: What if certain people in the man's life simply will not give him what he thinks he should expect? Let me offer some for-instances. What if the wife will always be too preoccupied with other things to notice some need the husband expects to be fulfilled? What if the kids never fully appreciate the efforts he makes on their behalf? Does this doom him to a life of angrily chastising the people nearest him for failing to meet his expectations? Of vainly seeking someone who will provide what he wants?

Having offered a question to think about and a challenge, I also provide a possible solution: "Angry man, acknowledge to yourself that you have inherent value regardless of the opinions and actions of fallible humans. It is God, through giving you the gift of life, who determines your worth. No human needs to be allowed to have the power of God over your inner opinions about self. *No one.*"

This leads to the second suggested solution: "When your anger boils up, communicate with the same respect you wish to receive." Certainly, the man has the option of continuing to let anger generate aggressive or passive behavior. Not good options. But if he, perhaps with help from you, can rein it in and develop new habits—assertiveness, boundary recognition, calm firmness—both will benefit immeasurably.

And much of the evasiveness that so commonly accompanies anger in men will dissolve.

**2. Control Issues.** When a wife tries to help the husband see how he is using control, or rather misusing it, the point may or may not reach home. All too often, controlling husbands (and wives) fail to take the spouse's opinions seriously. But human nature being what it is, control tactics are almost always met with control tactics of one form or another. The wife may respond passively to a husband's control *on the surface.* Almost always, she's using her own subtle means of persuasion.

Some are easy to see. The husband gets loud, so the wife gets loud. He gives orders, she gives orders or brings up some past event to throw in his face. He gets stubborn, she entrenches.

But some are difficult to recognize as control tactics. He gets loud, so she gives him the silent treatment, throwing him off balance. He becomes obnoxious in her opinion, so the bedroom door slams, figuratively or perhaps even literally. He insists on a particular standard of behavior or action. She withholds it or "forgets."

It all becomes such a sophisticated game that the players don't realize they're locked into it. And the players become so skilled that they play without thinking. Happiness goes down the tubes, and the marriage suffers.

How do you pull the plug on that game and start a new, healthier one, especially if half the players want to stick to the old game?

For starters, the wife ought to keep in mind that she married into a partnership, not an army. It is not the general ordering the private around. It is two autonomous people working together synchronously. Autonomous. Each holding the power of choice. He can order and tell her what she "must" do. It is for her to choose to do or not to do that particular thing in his prescribed way.

How freeing that is, the cry, "I have the God-given privilege to be what I choose to be and think what I choose to think."

As I told Andrea, "When Keith gives you his list of have-tos and shoulds and had-betters, recognize that those are only his opinion. You have the privilege to decide whether to go along with his preferences or you may not. You may see some other course and pursue it."

Keith grimaced. "She already does." He still smarted about being locked out.

"But her behavior is a reaction to yours. A predictable reaction. I'm asking her to think and act independently, not tying her response to your behavior. Break this control, counter-control pattern that is so destructive for you both."

"No." Andrea shook her head. "It wouldn't work. He doesn't take kindly to my changing my brand of cleanser. You're asking—"

"His responses are not something you can control. You can control you. That's all. I'm not suggesting you become an uncooperative, irresponsible rebel. Choose responsibility. Choose being considerate. But make them your choices, not automatic counter-control measures. Stay out of the power play."

"But how can I make him look up to me?"

"There's that control again. It's not your job to *make* him see you in a positive light. If your lifestyle is appropriate, the response to it is his. If he continues with his controlling measures, that's his problem, not yours."

She still looked skeptical.

"Think of it this way: When you choose not to take the counter-control measures that increase his anger and fuel yours, you reduce the level of anger in your home significantly. Is that a goal you want?"

"You make it sound so simple."

"Please don't hear that! It's not simple. It's not easy. We're talking about changing ingrained patterns of behavior. Believe me, the rewards are worth the cost."

**3. Grief Issues.** With Keith, I asked two questions: One, "If you were an average kid and you received treatment (from peers, parents, or siblings) that you described to me that you received, how might that treatment have generated anger?" The second, "What in the world makes you think you're immune?"

There naturally followed, then, "Can you see now that some of the anger you experience in your marital relationship today is actually a holdover from earlier times? Your misdirected anger can mean that you are letting unresolved grief and disappointment steal your happiness today."

Keith found it very hard to deal with all this—he'd been developing bad habits of dealing with anger for a long time—but when he fell, he fell hard. He began one session by confessing, "I've done a lot of thinking about this stuff, you know? Especially the part where I'm transferring onto Andrea some anger from the past. Sometimes when she's really ranking on me, I can see myself talking back to my parents because they were ranking on me and I'd been doing the best I could."

How did that help Andrea? For the first time in his life, Keith apologized to her for yelling.

In the meantime, Keith decided to talk with his parents, who were still alive, about some of his childhood memories. He tactfully (well, tactfully for Keith) told them how he hurt when he recalled their parenting and communication patterns. He also forgave them and reminded them of the good that he recalled from his youth. His purpose in doing so was exactly that—to forgive them. He expected no other outcome.

They did not receive his visit well, or even his forgiveness, but he reported that a great burden lifted off him, and that surprised him. He realized afterward that the visit was more for his benefit than theirs, and in that regard it succeeded well.

But we must assume now that your husband is nowhere near experiencing the change of heart Keith did. Where does that put you?

Analyzing his past can give you some insight into his present behavior. Weigh those experiences of hurt or grief that may still be influencing his anger today. From what you know of his past, and can surmise from meeting his kin, do you suppose he was unnecessarily and excessively dominated? Ignored? Misunderstood? Abandoned (not just physically, but emotionally, as when his parents would leave him alone at too early an age)? Deceived? Abused? Insulted? Labeled?

To get past all this, if he ever does, he must confront the past openly and forgive. Frankly, most men don't. He may need to seek a counselor's help to sift through the issues. Until he lets go of past pain, his harsh or passive anger patterns will probably persist.

But now you know their roots! Now you know you are not the cause, you are simply the target. He may say you are making him angry. He probably even believes that; but the past is governing him. You need not take it personally the way you used to. And there is a chance your change of attitude will force change in him.

Anger is like handball played against a wall. If the player's angle changes relative to the wall, the ball doesn't bounce in the same direction it used to. If you change your position, he is going to have to alter his because it no longer bounces off you.

## The Anger Itself

Husbands like Keith and Gary, with evasive relating patterns at least partly rooted in anger, can take major steps forward when they admit the need to understand and restructure their patterns of anger management. They will benefit, their marriage will benefit, and you will benefit. I recommend two healthy steps to take.

Let's use Gary Sweeney as the example. Keith was already primed to make some changes. Gary was, to say the least, reluctant to look at the possibility that anger was playing a detrimental part in his life. He did not behave in the obvious ways that you immediately associate with "Anger! He's angry." His anger was displayed covertly, passively.

The man's first step is to commit to openness about his needs and feelings without being coerced or coercive. Openness is tough. It takes assertiveness, the ability to address personal issues in a way that is constructive for all people involved. That is, first recognize the anger and then let it out in a way that doesn't demean or make hostile the person to whom you're expressing it.

I explained to Gary, "Sometimes you're annoyed with Ruth, but instead of being open you play mind games with her. You'll withdraw or pout or be uncooperative. As a result, you never get really honest with her about the way you feel."

With Keith, of course, honesty wasn't a problem; oftentimes he was a little bit *too* honest. He accused and griped and complained and roared, but it didn't work any better than Gary's obstructionism. Both methods lack real communication, not to mention diplomacy. Neither assuages or resolves the situation.

"Let's go a different route," I suggested. "Why not try firmness and openness, but accompany it with noncoercive methods of speech?" Then pointing toward my throat I explained, "The key to your delivery is right here. Your tone of voice. Speak your convictions but without coercion or pleading or salesmanship in your voice. You owe it to yourself and to your wife to be straightforward about your needs, but I'm suggesting that you also leave her room to process her response in her own style and timing."

"We're talking about some pretty shadowy, behind-the-scenes stuff here." Gary didn't look hopeful. "Ruthie is in your face but not too sharp at seeing what's not in front of her. What if I try this and Ruthie doesn't respond? She can fly off the handle faster'n hangers tangle up in a closet. Combative, you know?"

"It's not your job to get her to understand your anger fully or correctly. You can only control your own communication of it. Once you're satisfied that you have spoken openly and constructively, don't get entangled in a debate about how she's supposed to feel at the moment. Hear her perspective if that will bring some calm, then move on."

Husbands and wives determined to make changes in their relationship will see the value of open exposure of their anger, but they will simultaneously choose to steer away from tit-for-tat exchanges that go nowhere.

A second big step in anger management is to forgive or accept those incidences where assertiveness (reasoned expression of anger) will not work. Each marriage has incidences when spouses will never fully see eye-to-eye. Accepting that reality reduces the frequency of frustrating, nonproductive behavior that chips away at marital harmony. As every couple knows, the list of potential marital differences is endless: You disagree on parental decisions, your social needs do not perfectly overlap, one spouse is messy while the other is a perfectionist, one is fatigued when the other is perky. Little things generate big ones. And anger.

Rather than letting differences feed painful conflicts, husbands and wives can make plenty of allowance for error or dissonance. To men like Gary and Keith, I ask that they accept the inevitability of the spouse's uniqueness, in other words, departure from the husband's expectations, even when it means accepting imperfection.

Mix together a man's bent toward performance, toward competition and with it expectations of perfection, plus the craving for control, and you begin to see how hard it can be to give the wife room to be herself. He notes something that he thinks needs changing, and he hungers like anything to change it.

Maybe Andrea doesn't clean house as thoroughly as Keith prefers. Gary and Ruth find themselves at loggerheads over relationships with in-laws. I asked Keith and Gary to be smart enough to know when an issue is so important that it warrants firm assertion, and then be willing to live with a less-than-perfect relationship. "Chances are," I tell every man, "she is required to accept unpleasant things about you too."

The wise man also lets forgiveness guide him as well. You have heard the admonition: "Don't let the sun go down on your anger." The choice to let go of bitterness, resentment, and nagging frustration is for the forgiver's good far more so than the forgivee's. When either you or your man cling to the things that bother you, you lose your effectiveness, not only in your marriage, but in virtually every other important area of your life and his.

The other side of this coin provides good news for you the wife. Whether or not your husband comes to terms with the meaning of his anger, you now see what's going on inside him. You needn't struggle in doubt or guilt. "What did I do to set him off *this* time?" "He blames me for this, and it must be true. And yet . . ." By knowing what's going on, you will be far less inclined to falsely accept the responsibility for his actions. And believe me, most wives do.

Too, as you become comfortable with the fact that his anger, even if it is directed at you, is not so much about you as about his own inner struggles, you can better resist the temptation to become defensive or to go overboard trying to mollify him. You ought to render him respect as your husband, certainly, but you cannot prop up his ego. That must be mended from the inside.

I also offer the man this prospect to think about: It is highly likely that his anger began building early, even before marriage, at an age when he did not have the ability to understand its meaning. Children become bothered or frustrated when a parent scolds, particularly if the scolding or discipline is perceived as unjust or too harsh for the infraction. Unkind treatment, merciless teasing—the disrespect and cutting-down start early. Of course they have no inkling of how those experiences are tied to the normal desire for affirmation.

Almost never do boys receive training or guidance in anger management. What advice they get, even from parents, is usually the wrong stuff. "Now, Johnny, you mustn't get angry. It's only teasing." "Don't you dare get angry with your [sister, mother, father, teacher, whoever]!" "*Real* Christians don't get angry." "Big boys don't [you fill in the blank]." Bad habits of inappropriate (such as passive noncooperation or tuning out) and abusive (loud and/or violent) expressions of anger begin to form early. So often the wife is led to believe she is generating all this hostility when in reality, she is simply the current, handy recipient of a behavior pattern that's been a long time building.

My challenge to the man: "Now that you're an adult, those habits have become refined and entrenched, but the good news is this: You now have the ability to understand the underlying reasons for your anger. Rather than letting this emotion continue its destructive patterns, damaging your important relationships and your life, you can learn to believe in yourself to such an extent that you do not have to angrily demand that others must affirm you."

I'll challenge the wife here also. When his anger reaches an abusive extreme, you have no obligation to sit and take it. As obvious as that thought may seem, I have talked with hundreds of women who play the enabler role by putting up with unacceptable levels of anger and rebellion. Many times, they are afraid to respond with logical consequences, yet that is what they must do.

The verbally abusive husband who flings out the shouts and insults, especially the physically abusive husband by his behavior, forfeits the right to live in a comfortable home with domestic privileges that the wife provides. She is wise to alter her lifestyle and his until he chooses a better path. Again I caution against meeting anger with anger. Escalation achieves nothing. I recommend a calm, firm resolve not to conduct business as usual in the face of inappropriate anger.

This brings up another positive step for the wife to use. When you recognize his anger (remember that not all anger responses are easily discernible; passive obstruction, for example, is not), ask, "What shall I do about *my* anger?" It's an important question. So far, you've been either stuffing it or letting it cut loose, and obviously, neither tactic has been working. In fact, that's a pretty good rough-and-ready way to detect anger in him; is it generating anger in you?

Rather than fight fire with fire, wrong with wrong, anger with anger, you can choose an alternate course. Recognize that there are at least three other sources of his anger, realizing that it's not as personal as he claims. Then decide where you want to go with this. You'll speak firmly and act decisively without stooping to a demeaning, degrading, or angry manner. Commit yourself to that. Communicate what you intend. Speak to your issues, act according to your convictions; but realize that it's not your job to convince him you're right. You're pursuing your course, and if he understands, it is his concern.

This, of course, doesn't mean that he's a lout and you walk on water. I certainly don't intend to imply that. In fact, in this next chapter, let's examine a problem wives often experience that trips them up in their attempts to keep the marriage barge floating smoothly. Let's examine the potential for open fretting.

## chapter 6

# Her Open Fretting

ynette Sandstrom stood in the middle of the family room floor and yelled to no one in particular, "Why is it, every time I get the house looking decent, you have to make another mess?" With a bit of thought, she decided on the current culprit. "Kirby, come here!"

From the back of the house came Kirby's voice. "It wasn't me!"

"Kirby . . . !"

"I'm not home!"

"Get in here!"

Most reluctantly, her fifteen-year-old son came wandering in and whined, "Mom, I didn't do it! Why should I have to clean it up?"

She waved toward the *Car and Driver* magazines strewed across the floor. "How did you know what I was talking about if you didn't do it?"

"Survival tactics, Mom. It doesn't matter what you're talking about specifically, you know? Soon as you say, 'Company's coming,' I grab a couple of CDs and some granola bars and hide in my room." He shrugged. "Keep my head low and stay outta the flak, 'cause for sure there's gonna be some."

Of all the impudence! "Your room is a good place for you. And don't come out until I tell you!"

He burst into a grin. "Thanks, Mom!" and ran off.

There stood Howard in the dining room doorway.

Lynette's fury had just doubled, and why not? "Did you hear what Kirby just said?"

"He's got a good point." Howard crossed to the magazines and began scooping them into an untidy pile. "If you'd lighten up, you'd be a lot happier."

"Lighten up!" Lynette was losing it again, and she hated that. But . . . "Why don't *you* clean the kitchen and do the cooking and vacuum the house and take the dog to the vet and stop at the grocery? Get the place looking good for our company. They'll be here in an hour. Then I'll tell you to lighten up, and let's see how *you* feel!" She paused. "Howard, you're not going to stack those magazines by the fireplace there, are you?"

"Why not? I'm not done with them yet."

"I just cleaned in here!"

"This is our family room, Lynn. We live here." He plopped the magazines down in a ragged little stack, stood up, and spread his hands. "I'm available. What needs doing?"

"Take out the garbage." She headed for the door to sweep the patio one more time. "I don't know why you can't see something obvious, like the kitchen trash can is full, without having to be reminded." She paused in the doorway. "And put those magazines out on the porch."

## THE FRUITS OF FRETTING

Lynette was a world-class fretter. Fretting, simply stated, is the tendency to dwell on problems past the point of constructive solution. It draws more attention to annoyances, particularly in the eye of the fretter, than those annoyances realistically deserve.

In short, it strips the "petty" out of "petty annoyance." The fretter focuses so heavily upon negatives, he or she (let's say she, since we're using Lynette as the example) temporarily loses the confidence that a more positive outlook can foster. That loss of confidence then slops over into other areas of life.

For example, a day later, Lynette and Howard were getting ready for church when Lynette stopped to study herself in the mirror. "I think I'm putting on weight. Howard, am I getting fat?"

Ominous silence.

"Howard?"

He straightened his tie and turned to her. "Why do you do that to me so much?"

"Do what?"

"Pick a fight. I'm getting pretty tired of it, Lynn."

"I am not picking a fight! I asked you objectively if you think I'm starting to gain a little. I didn't—"

"Great! So let's pretend I answer, 'Yeah, Babe, I notice you're getting a little chunky there.' Not only would you rip my head off and mail it to a third-world country, you'd go on a diet. And that means I'd be getting rice cakes three times a day because the last time you went on a diet, everybody did. The boys were feeling guilty about sneaking doughnuts after school."

"Howard, that's not—"

"And if I say, 'No, dear, you look just fine,' you say, 'I don't know why I bother to ask you anything. You're never honest with me.' So I don't offer any answer at all, and you blow up anyway. Well, this time you're going to have to fight all alone. The boys and I will be out in the car."

He left.

See the erosion of Lynette's confidence that her fretting generated? And the trouble it caused?

The fruits of fretting aren't pretty.

I find these undesirable fruits are multiplied by the way in which so many women fret—their tone of voice. That uniquely edgy, unpleasant, insecure tone just by itself greatly increases the likelihood that the husband will distance himself.

The habit is so easy to fall into. Lynette, for example, wanted her house in apple-pie order. Her husband and sons looked on apple pie as something to eat and figured that if stuff was more or less tidied up, it was in order. But that was a matter of opinion.

The heart of the matter was this: Lynette's irritability and negativity baited Howard's anger. Precipitated it. Encouraged it. Howard, then, withdrew. It was his basic response when he was angry. Her fretting, you see, set up the situation so that Howard would act exactly the way she said she did *not* want him to act, evasive and distant.

In this case, Lynette herself was the cause of her problem with Howard.

In my practice I see nothing more common than a woman's fretting as the excuse her husband offers for evasiveness and distance. Some men's comments:

- "She'll be okay, and then she'll get off on some toot. So I just back away."
- "I don't know what to do when she's like this, so I don't do anything."
- "Picky, picky, picky. It gets old in a hurry."
- "If she'd just speak normally, she'd probably get what she wants."

Why do women persist in their fretting behavior if it produces negative results? For one thing, they don't realize they are doing it, or they do it so frequently. For another, they don't realize the effects it causes. Too, it's an easy way of communication to slip into. Overattention to detail, particularly when that attention is negative, breeds even more overattention.

I find that below the obvious level, however, most women's reasons for falling into a fretting habit is the search for affirmation, consideration, or cooperation. These are legitimate desires, hard to argue against. Unfortunately, fretting does not achieve them.

## How Much of a Fretter Are You?

To grasp some idea about whether you are using the fretting mode of behavior too much, check the following items that describe you. If to you some of them don't seem to contribute to fretting, humor me.

_____ 1. Others (especially my husband) say that I sound annoyed or pleading when I ask for something or communicate some need.

_____ 2. Now that I think about it, I often make a point by asking frustrated questions: "Why do you always _____?" "Can't you just _____?" "When are you ever going to _____?"

_____ 3. I get irritable when my spouse ignores me or shows insensitivity, and I let it show.

_____ 4. Keeping up good appearances and making a favorable impression are important to me.

_____ 5. I think my life contains more stress than it ought to.

_____ 6. When I make mistakes or accidentally offend someone, I feel guilty about it even when I'm told I'm forgiven.

_____ 7. My schedule is loaded with too many commitments.

_____ 8. On occasion I experience one or more of these symptoms: Headache, nervous stomach, irritable bowel, or grinding teeth.

_____ 9. I'm good at worrying about things before they happen.

_____ 10. When my husband doesn't pay any attention to my feelings, I feel rejected.

_____ 11. I try to look more secure in public than I feel inside.

_____ 12. I can't let go of conflict as easily as some others can.

Because it is normal for a woman to let emotions lead the way, everyone checks a few of those statements. But if you checked, or thought about checking, six or more, it is likely that you allow your worries to overcome you to the extent that fretting plays too prominent a role in your behavior and communication. You can improve the quality of your married life by minimizing this tendency, choosing other paths instead.

Lynette admitted how she tended to fret according to the definition we laid down here. And she also admitted that it might be causing friction in her marriage. Beside her, Howard was bobbing his head in eager agreement.

She insisted, however, "But I wouldn't be like that if Howard would carry his half! I keep trying to deal with things, and he keeps backing away. If he'd simply try to understand and handle issues, I'd be so much happier."

"It sounds to me," I responded, "that you're dumping the burden of your emotional stability and happiness onto Howard's shoulders. That's risky and unfair."

Howard nodded enthusiastically.

That zipped right past her. "Let me show you what I'm talking about. Last night I asked Howard to help Kirby with his homework, and what do I get? A nasty jab, but no help. He wouldn't—"

"Now hold on!" Howard broke in. "Let's get the full picture here. You and Kirby were waltzing around for half an hour about how he couldn't do this and couldn't do that unless he got his math done first. All it was, his idea of his evening's schedule didn't match up exactly to yours. You made a federal case out of twenty minutes of Nintendo after supper. He could have had his math finished in the time you took chewing on him. Then you turned on me and griped about how I made matters worse by not speaking up. All I was doing was staying out of the cross fire."

She looked livid. "That seems to be the basic mode of operation in our house. Keep your head down. Don't bother to accept any responsibility; let Lynn carry it all. I wasn't asking for the moon." She turned to me. "One of Kirby's trigonometry questions was how to measure the height of a tree. Mr. Helpful here says to me, 'Well, you could go climb it.' They both thought that was just hilarious. I'm still furious!"

Sometimes in a counseling session it's very, very hard to keep from laughing.

## 🌊 *FACTORS IN FRETTING—AND REVERSING THEM*

Let's take apart the situations that gave Lynette such fits and see how they might have been managed more profitably.

Wives usually fall into a pattern of fretting when they are overburdened by one or more of these three factors: taking on too much responsibility, feeling victimized, and clinging to idealism. They link together. Let's look at them.

### The Fretting Factors and How They Function

It seems strange to suggest that some women can possess too much of a sense of responsibility. In this day and age, when self-indulgence and irresponsibility seem to be so prevalent, surely we must need more, not fewer, people who maintain a strong work ethic. Every person who arranges his or her priorities wisely and then sticks to them is a blessing on humankind. There can never be a shortage of people living a strongly responsible lifestyle, can there?

As is the case with any positive trait, it is possible to have too much of a good thing. This is the situation with most fretting wives. Life can and will present its share of inconsistencies, mysteries, and disappointments. For any number of reasons, these women feel a strong sense of responsibility to make certain everything in their world turns out exactly right. Because nothing in this world ever turns out exactly right, they become more desperate to achieve the impossible and impose greater and greater responsibility upon themselves, trying to get the whole world to march to their specific beat. The fretting woman spends *so* much time trying to force life to be what it is not!

Let's take an example from Lynette's past. Because she felt the school cafeteria served too much fat and starch, she packed carefully balanced lunches for her sons. The boys dutifully toted their lunches off to school. In the cafeteria, they swapped the apples for Twinkies, the tuna sandwiches for pizza, and the nutritionally sound, homemade cookies for baseball cards. Sometimes these trades were not altogether welcomed by the other trading parties—smaller kids who gave up their Twinkies because they knew better than to argue with the big guys. The rice cakes went into the garbage. They couldn't even trade rice cakes to first graders. When Lynette found out, she hit the roof.

And I am certainly not belittling Lynette's attitude or the admirable goal behind it—to provide her children with the best nutrition. I'm simply showing that sometimes life isn't going to cooperate.

Very frequently the husband does not share the wife's aims and goals for perfection. She then assumes that he is abrogating his responsibility. In reality, he simply wanted to take a different course.

I'm thinking now of a couple who came to me on the brink of separation because of their thirteen-year-old daughter. Let's call the wife Laura, her husband Frank, and the daughter Bethany. Bethany was not present at this session when we discussed her.

Laura explained, "When we enrolled Bethany in a private Christian school, we thought she was safe from the really dangerous influences. But there's a group of girls who are pretty wild, and the school isn't doing anything about it. Cigarettes and alcohol, and I suppose pot. I don't want Bethany anywhere near that clique."

Being a dad of a teenager myself, I understood and agreed with those concerns. Many young girls are easily swayed as they attempt to fit into an adult life that isn't really geared for them.

Laura wanted to uphold her parental responsibility of instilling strong moral values in her daughter. Good!

But then she demonstrated how a good quality can be taken too far as she added, "There are girls in her class I don't even want her to talk to."

Beside her, Frank threw up his hands in a what's-the-use gesture.

"See?" Laura bristled. "Frank, I don't think you really care the way you say you do about our child's future. You certainly aren't taking any responsibility to direct it."

Frank appealed to me. "Whenever I suggest anything short of her hard-line secret-police tactics, she harps at me as if I'm a complete idiot. Either I take her extreme stance or she's not interested in discussing it. There's no middle ground with her."

And so I asked Laura, "Could it be that your sense of responsibility for your daughter's behavior is so strong that you're pressing too hard?"

"How can a parent feel too strongly about her teenage daughter's moral development?" Her tone of voice was irritated and defensive.

I wanted to create a calmer atmosphere here, and I also wanted to separate out the two factors that Laura was mistakenly combining into one: her desire for her daughter's well-being and her extreme need to implement that desire her way. "We're not discussing the values you and Frank hold. I suspect you two are in nearly total agreement on that. Rather, I'm looking at the tactics you're using and what their effects are. You're trying to control every detail of your daughter's life, things that cannot possibly be controlled, such as to whom she talks, and you're also trying to control your husband's actions. You want him to support your stance in every single way, even though he disagrees with your methods. See the problem here?"

"You have to fight for what's right!"

"Absolutely! We're agreed. Let's look at the means and methods. So far, in what ways has your fight improved your marriage?"

"What . . . ?"

"Your husband is your most powerful ally in that fight. How are you encouraging him?"

"He doesn't care."

"That's not true!" The way it burst out of Frank, you could tell how angry he was.

And so we went round and round. It took a long, hard pull to help Laura realize that she was trying to force not a moral standard onto Frank but her own peculiar notion of responsibility.

He knew the first rule of parenting: "Control what you can control, and don't try to control what you cannot control."

He also wanted to help Bethany develop her own self-discipline, not try to impose it upon her rigorously from outside. Laura had a hard time with both of those concepts. They sounded great in theory, but they butted up against her powerful sense of responsibility to make the world march to her drummer. Also, note how she was striving for an unattainable ideal of controlling every detail of her daughter's life. And she was hinging her happiness upon achieving that ideal!

I call this grasping at idealism *mythical thinking*. The woman is hoping against all odds—impossible odds—that her fantasy will come true exactly as she wants it to. You can see how that can set a person up for disappointment and its resulting irritability.

And look at beleaguered Lynette Sandstrom. See the responsibilities she took upon herself to bring to fruit an ideal? Her ideal was a perfectly arranged home in which four vigorous people were supposed to live neatly coordinated lives. The ideal can be approached but not achieved. That didn't stop her from idealizing her desires, then fretting when they didn't happen. It didn't stop her from continuing to try to achieve the impossible.

One of the questions I asked her to consider was, "Why do you think Howard and the boys have independently developed a policy of keeping their heads down?"

If you analyze the examples I cited in this chapter, you can see that the fretting method is very much based upon guilt. I would say it is driven by guilt. The fretter feels guilt and uses guilt trips to coerce the frettee, if you will, into cooperating.

I asked Laura on one occasion about the methods her own mother used to promote desired behavior.

Her immediate response: "Guilt trips! Mothers have a rep, I know, for laying guilt on you, but my mom was the gold medalist."

When I asked the same question of Lynette, her answer was, "Mom could make you feel guilty just by the way she puckered her eyebrows. I've never seen anything like it."

Ruth's parents did not use guilt to any extent as a coercive method, apparently, but Gary's mom certainly did, and Ruth picked up more than one habit from her mother-in-law, with whom she was quite close. Guilt trips, like viruses, are infectious.

Using guilt and assuming false guilt are two problems to guard against. Almost always, false guilt is at the root of the guilt trip one spouse lays upon another. False guilt harms. It never enlightens or improves. Guilt for not achieving an impossible ideal is some of the worst.

As guilt deserves attention in your life, so does this factor of idealism. Like guilt, it lies unseen behind fretting behavior, driving that fretting as with a whip. Beneath the nagging and the fussiness lies the unspoken complaint: "I can't believe I have to live with such imperfection!"

Can you identify places in your life where impossible idealism and an exaggerated sense of responsibility may be causing friction?

## The Fallout from Control-by-Fretting

Here are some situations I've run across more than once in counseling. They illustrate ways in which the wife assumes a certain level of responsibility, perhaps a very high ideal, and tries to move her husband toward adopting her attitude. Were you to adapt these situations to your marriage and your circumstances, substituting words here and there but keeping the context, would they apply to you?

- You believe your husband should be more winsome and extroverted in social gatherings, so you urge him to mix more, to talk more, to not hide behind the punch bowl, etc.
- Your husband is not assuming the parental role you expect of him, so you detail how you want him to improve.
- You believe your husband should have a closer rapport with your extended family, so you advise him of ways to achieve this, even though he certainly didn't ask.
- When you plead with him regarding some matter you want him to correct or improve, he says you're whining.

I trust you get the idea.

Now here's what happens as you pursue your goals.

As Frank explained to Laura, "I'm a conscientious father. I love Bethany and try to guide her in the ways I feel will work best. You won't recognize that. You don't accept that I might be doing all right. You don't trust me to be an adequate parent."

*You don't trust me.*

Laura stammered that, well, of course, that's not true; certainly she trusted him, but . . . but . . . It hit her right between the eyes.

Howard to Lynette: "I got along fine for twenty years before I met you. Why do you think that now I can't do anything unless you direct? Why can't you trust me to live my own life instead of picking at me to do everything your way?"

*You don't trust me.*

Laura and Lynette both frequently used questions such as these to hammer home a point:

"What's wrong with you?"

"Where did you ever come up with that idea?"

"How can you [do, say, think] that?"

These sorts of comments are loaded questions, of course, not asked for the purpose of gaining insight but for making the opposing viewpoint look foolish. The wife's message: *I don't even trust you to exercise normal intelligence.*

I don't have to discuss the fact everyone knows: A successful marriage cannot exist without trust.

There is one other unhappy by-product that deserves mention here, and it's the one that Ruth and Gary kept bumping into. So did Lynette and Howard, for that matter. The woman's fretting, irritating for the above reasons as well as for the cranky, impatient tone of voice so often used, unites the husband and the kids in a clique defending themselves against (or avoiding) Mom. "There goes Mom on another of her rampages. We must band together against her unreasonableness." It may not be said aloud, but it's the unspoken message.

Good, effective parenting unites mother and father in a team to uplift the kids. Fretting destroys that team. Laura was defeating her own purposes. So was Lynette. So was Ruth.

## The Problem of Victimization

The other factor, a feeling of being victimized, rides on the backs of excessive responsibility and unreachable ideals. Did you hear Lynette in the incident that opened the chapter? Listen to what she was really saying:

"I have to do all this work, and you people don't even care that you always undo what I have done. I'm the only one here who thinks about impressing our guests. I'm the only one with an adequate sense of responsibility."

In a nutshell, *Poor me! I'm being victimized!*

Now understand there are certainly many wives who are genuinely victimized. Their husbands have indeed abrogated responsibility. Some husbands really are insensitive, abrasive, or tuned out. Some wives suffer greatly because of their husbands' physical, verbal, or emotional abuse, their husbands' extramarital affair, extreme financial mismanagement, and so on. I'm sure you can cite such instances among your friends. This is all very real victimization, and I agree that it's the husband's doing. But . . .

When any two imperfect people live together for any extended period of time, it is highly probable that one will suffer grief because of the other's inadequacies. No one is immune, and the person suffering can lay a legitimate claim to victimization.

But in this chapter on fretting, I'm talking about the victimization the wife can bring upon herself. In her case, her distant husband has been pushed to that distance, at least in part, by her fussing and fretting. To that extent she is her own victim.

She does not help her case by voicing her victimization, even in indirect ways:

- "Nobody picks up after themselves. I'm constantly cleaning up junk!"
- "My husband is proud of the work he does in the kitchen occasionally. He doesn't realize I have to go in behind him and do it over again right."
- "If I left town for a week, this place would fall apart!"

However, the victim has every right to attempt to redress the problem. Gary and Ruth provide a good example here. Soon after they married, Gary started making cutting comments about Ruth in front of the relatives. Ruth didn't like it. Gary's response: "It's just family. They all know it's not true." Before long, though, he was doing it in any social group, getting laughs at Ruth's expense, denigrating her. She tried responding in-kind, and now she's very good at cut-cut.

When Ruth recognized the recurring situation for what it was—verbal warfare—she confronted Gary (as he was coming out of the shower one night so he couldn't escape!) and declared an end to it. When next it happened, she reminded him in front of everyone that he had promised he wouldn't do that. Two such well-placed reminders snuffed the habit.

So realizing that you are being victimized does have its value. It can be the basis from which you work for positive change.

But again, you can carry a good thing too far. As in the case of being too responsible, it is also possible to cling too strongly to the victim status. Some wives go so far as to build their identities around their role as victim, their feelings of victimization. Anxiety and fretting always result.

Every person feels victimized and at times, justifiably. How about you? Such feelings taken to excess become a problem. Is it a problem with you?

- Do you collapse at times under feelings of hopelessness or disillusionment?
- Do you feel paralyzed and hopeless about controlling your own destiny and providing for yourself a reasonably good future?
- Do you pretty much expect things to go wrong in your relationship?
- Do you assume you have no choices regarding the quality of your life?

If you recognize any of these tendencies in yourself, you are probably carrying an unnecessary burden of feeling victimized. Your problems have defined who you are.

As Laura, the beleaguered mother of Bethany, said once, "I dread having to do anything with Frank that requires coordinated efforts. He just doesn't understand organization and how to harmonize efforts, do you know what I mean? He doesn't have the slightest idea how I prefer to operate."

"And so," I responded, "you start out a project assuming you're going to be disappointed. What are the chances of this becoming a self-fulfilling prophecy?"

She looked woebegone. "Probably 100 percent."

As we talked the idea over, Laura began to see that she went into any joint project with Frank assuming she would be hurt emotionally in some way. She even began looking for ways in which Frank was going to make her miserable. Frank was one of those individuals you would call "a difficult person." No doubt about it. He acknowledged as much. But Laura was so predisposed to her victim role that she convinced herself before the fact that she would be hurt and would begin feeling edgy before anything occurred. Her edginess translated into fretting and irritation.

## Taking a New Course

Laura, Lynette, and Ruth all could see the factors that led to their fretting behavior. That's the first step in taking a new course. Perhaps by now you also can see these factors at work in your life. You, too, have just taken the first step.

The second step is to modify not your spouse's behavior but your own. It's a well-proven adage that when two sides are locked in a mutually dependent behavior pattern, if one side changes, the other cannot remain the same.

The precept of parenting also works here: Control what you can control; don't try to control what you cannot control. The wife can control her own responses and behaviors. She cannot effectively control her spouse's.

For starters, then, maintain a positive demeanor.

What constitutes a positive demeanor? Being firm, calm, and even cheerful, if possible. This sort of thing is easy to do when everything is going smoothly. It's not easy to do when irritation and tension are mounting. But the woman who can remember this manner of response and keep with it will see an immediate difference in herself and possibly also in her spouse.

As I told Laura, "You can maintain that firm, sweet demeanor regardless of Frank's level of cooperation or behavior. Instead of reacting to his behavior, you go your own course. You are essentially taking the lead."

She looked dubious. Victims don't lead, as a general rule. It would require a change in self-talk on her part.

We discussed specific things she could do:

- She could state her needs without feeling required to back them up with numerous justifications.
- If Frank were in a bad mood, she need not take upon herself the duty to cajole him out of it. And she need not always alter her plans to try to ease or accommodate his grumpiness.

- She could devise a good plan and follow through with it, whether she enjoyed his total endorsement beforehand or not.
- When making a request, she would avoid repeating the same point over and over, trying to enlist his cooperation.

These proactive behaviors are contrary to the usual reactive victim behavior. You can't maintain them and keep the victim persona.

Moreover, fretting implies not only that the wife feels victimized but that she lacks confidence in herself. She cannot make her spouse treat her the way she wants, but she can take her own plans and ideas seriously. By developing that mind-set, the wife, you see, is not obligated to remain a feckless victim.

What about you? Will you remain in the mode of bemoaning the unfair treatment you receive, or will you move forward with healthy actions and choices?

## Understand that Idealism May Not Always Be Served

"Peachy," Ruth grumbled. "Gary isn't the father I want him to be, so I'm supposed to settle for mediocrity."

Gary grumbled just as darkly, "You coulda phrased that a lot better."

"Okay, how's this? When Mr. Noninvolvement here turns evasive or tunes me out, I'm supposed to just shrug it off and pretend it doesn't bother me? Well, it does!"

I asked her, "So far, how well have your efforts succeeded in making Gary into the perfect father you envision?"

"Okay, so they haven't. Does that mean I quit trying?"

"If it's not working, why cling to it?"

"True." But she looked far from convinced. "What do I do instead?"

"Good question!"

Denying one's feelings is damaging. Pretending you like something unlikable is certainly no solution. Accepting a dose of reality is. The next step for these women is to rethink ideals that have consistently gone unmet.

Let's take Laura and Frank as the example. A reality check shows Laura that Frank has not shaped up according to her ideal. Frank is probably never going to be exactly what she wants. Now what?

Laura has two choices. She can continue trying to force him into the mold he is so consistently resisting, or she can accept reality. That involves reshaping her expectations. Then as a final step, she can work around the new expectations, restructuring her own behavior and attitudes to mesh better with reality.

The first choice, continuing the battle, causes pain and a sense of loss along with frustration and anger.

Frankly, so does the second. Laura is dulled to the pain of the first choice because she's been at it so long. That makes the second choice frightening and very hard to accept because she knows the pain will come, and it will be fresh.

Often women embroiled in this problem come from a family with a history of extremes. One such extreme is the family in which the children were catered to. Lynette was raised in such a family. Mother attended to Lynette's every need and Daddy to her every whim. They adjusted to her. She grew up assuming that relationships should be relatively pain-free, and that people who love you minimize any situation that might be uncomfortable. It was an unspoken expectation, the "natural" thing.

Howard, of course, didn't know about it.

The other extreme is a history of childhood unhappiness and tension. The family was dysfunctional to the point of keeping the child in turmoil. The daughters console themselves with the dream, "Someday it will be different!" They enter marriage expecting the new husband, who is not a part of the family that caused so much unhappiness, to provide the life of comfort and peace that they long for.

The white knight doesn't have a clue that he should be fixing all the old wounds. Therefore he only disappoints, and he doesn't have a clue to that, either.

Can a big swig of reality help? Yes!

The reality is, it is impossible to avoid pain. So many people float in a fantasy that this reality is not a reality at all.

"For crying out loud," Ruth would fume. "I've known pain my whole life. Of course it's unavoidable!"

But this came as a revelation to Lynette. She had bought wholesale into the pain-avoidance myth. Back talk from the boys, Howard's disinterest in her activities, his priorities as opposed to hers—it all hurt. She experienced a life-changing breakthrough when she realized, "These things are not going to disappear simply because I want them to. Looks like I may have to make some room for them."

I urged Lynette to implement that new attitude by accepting ugly reality in small things. Practice, as it were. As she became accustomed to identifying small unpleasantries and encouraging herself to roll with the punches, big ones did not seem quite so overwhelming.

This is, obviously, a matter that depends strongly on the woman's personality and prior approach to pain and unpleasantness. For a woman like Ruth, this would not be a significant thing. For Lynette it was gargantuan. Each woman must deal with pain according to her own background. For some it will be less daunting. But it will be difficult for any.

As each woman chooses deliberately not to spend excessive energy on the small stuff, she will find the inner strength to face the larger stuff, the things you cannot simply blow off. I believe that every woman is born with the strength to overcome adversity. She has to find and exercise it.

What is the outcome? The more you acknowledge your ability to work with reality instead of mythical thinking, the less inclined you will be to try to force compliance from your spouse. Certainly, you will still speak openly about things that bother you. But your happiness no longer hinges upon achieving an illusory perfection. A healthy skepticism will remind you that people and circumstances will, sooner or later, invariably disappoint. And that includes your spouse. It is not your job to perfect others. Your job is to respond with your own personal stability, to work through life on an even keel.

## Choosing the Course

"So I just keep my mouth shut?" Lynette wasn't about to keep her mouth shut, rest assured.

"Fortunately, no," I responded.

That's taking attempts to adjust to the wrong extreme. For her own good, the wife needs to make her needs and wishes known. The vast majority of husbands really do want to help their wives to happiness. They can't do that unless they know what works and what doesn't. Unless she tells her man of her wants and needs, he will remain oblivious to them.

But I strongly recommend *telling*, not *insisting* or even *imploring*. No crabbing, no justifications, no nit-picking. Send the ball to his court. If he returns, you're ahead. If he lets it by, you are no further behind.

Too, such requests, even when made without fretting or coercion, may not "stick." They may be treated as a request of the moment and not a request to change a pattern. Let's use Gary and Ruth as the example.

Gary is not a slob, but neither is he a neatnik. He gets home from a hard day's work and unwinds instantly, leaving behind a trail of work boots, leather gloves, coffee mug, shirt, socks, newspaper as he moves through the house. Ruth asks him to pick up after himself, using no insistent pleading or fretful manner. He does so.

The next day, he gets home from work and leaves another trail of personal items. In other words, Ruth's request worked on the one occasion only. She asks again, pointing out that she hopes he can develop a habit of picking up after himself. The next day, though, is no better. He simply doesn't remember and is in no mood to make the effort to change.

Ruth can now follow one of two possible courses. She can make an issue of it and, with even voice and reasoned communication, try to work a change. Or she can accept that this is Gary and save her efforts for bigger issues.

There is a key. Pick your battles carefully. Save the big guns for the truly important matters. To Ruth, Gary's greater involvement as a parent was tremendously important. So it would be wise for her to back off lesser things and hold her ground on the big one.

By blowing off minor issues, the wife shows with her actions that she is not so consumed by her own preferences that she cannot bend. What constitutes a minor issue? Something that probably won't matter much in the long run.

Here is another key: Allow your spouse the room to follow his own convictions. Laura did not, remember. Her adamant assumption that her approach was the only right one, and the hostility that attitude engendered, wrecked her chances of winning her husband to her side. It very nearly wrecked her marriage, and it unfavorably colored her opinion of her husband.

In summary, therefore, your goal is to declare your needs and feelings in a way that will result in the greatest degree of consideration, assuming he will consider those requests at all. Be firm, be succinct. Then allow him the privilege of choosing how he will respond. Refraining from nit-picking, salesmanship, and excessive complaining will benefit your cause. With his masculine mind-set, he is most likely to consider your thoughts when you show temperance and the strength to follow your own course.

# $\mathcal{H}$is Buried Insecurity

$\mathcal{A}$s a fisherman, Gary Sweeney made a good bull-dozer operator, but that didn't keep him from trying to fish. He gave up on fly-fishing early on. He was too impatient to stand around for hours with cold feet, flicking the line here and there. He soured on bottom fishing when a catfish spiked him. Ah, but bass. Now that was a different story! Not only did he enjoy a modicum of success, there was always something to do. Make your crank bait do tricks, try different holes, sit and doze.

His bass fishing buddy was, believe it or not, called Bubba. Bubba had an annoying habit of boasting on the yard-long stripers that teemed back home in Oklahoma lakes and denigrating anything under five pounds. But Gary learned a lot about fishing from the highly skilled Bubba and immensely enjoyed the cheerful Okie's effusive company.

Bubba could talk cars, anything from Formula One to Chevy pickups, and probably had a tattoo of Snake Prudhomme somewhere on his body. He was an astute observer of men and women, and on those occasions when he got serious, usually toward the end of the day and always in private, he provided deep insights. To Bubba, life was an adventure, and he wanted you to come along for the ride.

A phone call from Bubba, "Hey, Fox-man, let's go fishing," was about the only thing that could lure Gary away from his heavy work schedule.

One of Bubba's million-or-so friends owned a fifteen-acre ranch pond in a heavily wooded tract. In return for unlimited fishing privileges, Bubba stocked the pond himself with, of course, largemouth bass and feeder fish that just happened to be good pan fish in their own right. Without being asked to, he also maintained the pond as prime habitat.

Today Gary quit work a few hours early. Bubba borrowed Gary's one-ton pickup and together they sank a load of weighted tires at the south end of the pond to provide extra cover for hatchlings. They then spent the balance of the afternoon and evening trying to outwit sleeping lunkers. Conditions were ideal—overcast, seventy degrees, just enough breeze to ripple the surface.

Gary felt about as close to heaven as a person can get without ceasing breathing. He thought the world of Bubba, and it didn't hurt a bit that Bubba held Gary in high esteem. The name *Fox-man* originated from Bubba's claim that, "Gary Sweeney can teach a thing or two about digging to foxes and gophers." Now they sat at either end of a bass boat, with their cooler and its beverages, sandwiches, and live bait nestled in the middle where both could reach it easily. It was going to be another hour before anything serious started biting, but who was counting?

Gary cast out into a pool at the roots of an overhanging cottonwood. "How's your father doing, Bub?"

"Poorly. Open heart surgery sure ain't nothing to write songs about, and he's got some complications going." Bubba dipped a scull and edged the boat in closer to the reeds along the shore.

"Deb's getting a little cranky over it. Wound up tight as a garage door spring. You and Ruthie argue much?"

"Average, I guess." Gary shrugged. "Depends how the kids are doing mostly. When they're having problems, she gives me problems."

Bubba abandoned the reeds and tried near some willows. "I hear ya. Shucks, I do what I can. Run errands for Deb, even watch the kids sometimes when she goes into the hospital to see him or take him something. It's never enough, though, to hear her talk. She says I make such a big deal out of helping around the house that she'd just as soon I didn't bother. Crabby."

Gary turned to look at him. "Don't you ever go into the hospital and see him too?"

"Naw. Too depressing."

"Sheesh! How do you manage to get out of it? If that was my father, Ruthie'd drag me in by the ears."

"Deb tried to." Bubba reeled his lure slowly, with almost forced casualness. "What if he died while I was there? I couldn't stand that. Or to see him with all them tubes and hoses in him, when I remember how he used to be. Deb just don't understand, and I ain't about to explain it to her." He glanced at Gary. "Your pappy died, right?"

"Couple of years ago. Cancer. One day he's doing fine, and six months later we're tossing dirt on his casket. I understand what you're saying, about them wasting away. I wanted to talk about it with Ruthie, but somehow I just couldn't. She thinks I didn't care much. She still doesn't know how deep it ripped me up."

Bubba nodded. "Neither does Deb. And she ain't about to."

## ⪜ HIDDEN INSECURITY

Most men instantly understand the scene above and relate to it. Gary and Bubba were exchanging information probably no one else in the world would ever hear. Most women respond with, "For heaven's sake, why don't you just say how you feel?"

Men need to look good to the world emotionally. That's not "want to." That's "need." They need to know that they're not a flop in some major area—for most men, minor areas as well. Even more, they need for no one to suspect they're less than perfect in some area. They cannot admit to imperfection or emotional vulnerability.

But there is an added dimension to all this. Deep inside, nearly all men fear that they have somehow tripped up, big time, or that they are about to. They have been conditioned to assume that their worth will be depleted if they are somehow shown to be less than ideal.

That's insecurity.

Bubba, competent and successful in so many ways, lived in terror of the possibility that he would collapse emotionally as his father neared death. He had to distance himself and keep a tight rein on his feelings to avoid the emotional closeness that he feared might be his undoing. He hoped his father would understand. For sure, his Deb did not.

Gary buried his emotions when he buried his father. It was the only thing he knew to do with them to keep them from making him look foolish or weak. In all this, he felt extremely foolish and weak. The more powerfully his father's death assailed him, the more he had to erect a barrier to appear strong. In the end, he could not even lower the barrier for the one person who would have understood, his Ruth.

This fear of failure and fear of appearing to be a failure inhibits and damages the marital relationship because, by and large, the wife does not understand or sympathize, let alone empathize. She sees the distancing and lack of communication as lack of caring, as evasiveness. After all, if she were the one behaving this way, her behavior would be driven by callousness, not insecurity. It seems reasonable, she assumes, that his must be.

Remember that the man hiding insecurities does not necessarily look as if he feels insecure about anything. Feelings of inadequacy may never show. Like Bubba, he's the picture of competency. Like Bubba, that's not the man deep inside. I've seen many men in counsel who display a very powerful persona, the look of success, and a confident manner of speech, yet who harbor severe hidden insecurities.

Nearly every man hides feelings of insecurity to some degree. Usually it's not a problem. But for the distant, evasive husband, buried insecurities may be causing that distancing in part.

To analyze the prospect that buried insecurities could be posing a problem, may I suggest you check the statements below that pertain to your husband and marriage. Remember that most men display many of these signs to a limited extent. That's natural. Rather, we're looking for excessiveness.

_____ 1. Through the years, I've found reason to suspect that my husband harbors secrets from me and others.

_____ 2. He takes great pains to present an image that is as blemish-free as possible.

_____ 3. When I try to talk about a problem regarding feelings, either his or mine, he appears uncomfortable and evasive about discussing personal topics in-depth. He'll explore the problems of anyone else in the world before he'll discuss his own.

_____ 4. He has to have the answers, no matter what the problem, whether he can offer reasoned, legitimate answers or not.

_____ 5. He gets irritable in reaction to unusual or unwarranted situations.

_____ 6. He likes to point out the shortcomings of others.

_____ 7. He rarely if ever lets his guard down in a social situation. He keeps most of his conversations at a shallow level.

_____ 8. I've come to see that his demeanor on the outside looks much more controlled and calm than I know him to be on the inside.

_____ 9. His eagerness for sex sometimes overwhelms or frustrates me.

_____ 10. He seems to dwell upon any little success and tries desperately to hide any little failure.

_____ 11. He expects elevated, favored treatment from me and the kids.

_____ 12. He seems to always need a little bit more, whether it be more affection, more positive recognition, or more financial security.

I repeat that it's abnormal for a man to show none of the above. If you checked six or more, however, there is a good probability that your husband feels more insecure, deep inside, than do most men. And that might be one cause of his distancing.

Neither Bubba nor Gary would call their failure to discuss deep feelings and fears dishonesty. In a sense, though, that's exactly what it is. It's not the true self. It's a false front, carefully constructed to hide what they consider a shoddy structure.

Picture Gary building a house across the span of his thirty-three years. At first, others govern the shaping of it, and frankly, they make mistakes. All builders do. But as years go by, Gary adds his own rooms, taking over construction himself. He corrects some others' mistakes and makes some of his own, but as his skill grows, his house becomes more interesting and more useful. What results is a charmingly eccentric, unique home. But Gary is embarrassed, even say shamed, because he feels it is not perfect. He fears that neighbors will not like living so close to this weird house. Passersby will laugh or sneer.

And so he uses his skills honed over a lifetime to build a giant facade across the front of it. As you stand out on the street looking at it, you see the perfect Victorian home, with three colors of paint, lots of gingerbread, the big porch, even a widow's walk. It looks like every other painted lady—very nice, but actually quite ordinary as Victorians go. Behind that facade, though, lies a one-of-a-kind house that would extol Gary's unique gifts if only he would not be ashamed of them.

One more item in the picture: Gary makes Ruth stay out on the street, just as Bubba keeps Deb outside. They never let the wives see behind the facade because they are too close and are supposed to think the facade *is* the house and perfection is the rule.

Gary occasionally allows his close friend Bubba to see behind the mask. Just as there is that need to look good, there is a need almost as compelling to say, "Look what I built! This is the real house. See the depth and uniqueness! Not shallow like the facade at all."

Bubba is perceived as "safe," in part because he shares the need to mask insecurity. Ruth is not; she lets feelings and insecurities hang unashamedly out in the open. And that is what damages the marriage relationship.

What is a wife to do?

When I counsel men and their wives in situations where buried insecurities have become a real problem in the marriage, I see two trends frequently: a history of conditional love in the marriage and before it, and a lack of trust bonds. The wife can do much to alleviate both those influences.

## Conditional Love

We have already seen that performance dominates the life of a man from boyhood on. Even small boys quickly become aware that they are evaluated according to what they do or do not do. From childhood they learn to cover up anything deemed negative and showcase the positive. You can see how that feeds the hiding of insecurities. But it also lays a solid foundation for conditional love—love and approval based solely on what shows on the surface.

Gary and I talked about that.

In response to my questions Gary said, "You bet! My daddy left his personal problems at the back door when he walked into the house. And you sure as blazes didn't air any laundry in public, dirty or otherwise. Private meant private with a capital P.

"To my dad, showing anger was almost as bad as talking about fears and problems. I learned early to hide it. And I have a real problem with anger too. I boil over fast. Everybody says how mellow I am and how I roll with the punches and don't get bent out of shape. Guys say they like working for me because I don't cloud up and rain all over them. But inside I'm screaming my brains out."

"Your father shaped you powerfully."

"He was a powerful man. 'Course, you weren't allowed to be angry in church either. Or at school. You know: the right image."

I knew. "In other words, you learned that in order to be accepted by the people you wanted to be accepted by—"

"That was pretty much the whole world, but mostly my dad."

I nodded. "You had to display the correct qualities, and anger wasn't one of them. We're using anger as an example, but there were other qualities also. You learned early on that love has conditions placed upon it."

"Never thought of it that way." He mulled all this a moment. "So you're saying that I wouldn't let my parents and sisters see certain things because it was too risky. I might not be loved."

"Exactly. Conditional acceptance."

"Man, you don't know the half of it." Gary smirked. "I was thirty years old before I found out that perfectly normal men think about sex a lot. I was sure I was weird and maybe even one of those potential criminals. All those years I'm thinking to myself, 'Sweeney, you are over the edge. Don't you ever let your family know how perverted you are.'"

"Now let's take that a step further. Ruth is as much family as are these others from whom you hide your true self."

"So I'm programmed, you might say, to keep stuff from her too."

"Programming is an excellent word for it. And she interprets that not as a lifetime of programming but as either lack of caring or distancing on your part. She probably takes it personally, in fact. Of course," I added, "it is important to the husband to look great in the eyes of his woman. So there's that element as well."

Gary sighed. "How come life can't be simple?"

We all ask that!

## Easing the Problem of Conditional Love

Gary, Bubba, and so many others were reaping what others had sown. They felt totally at sea concerning ways to reverse their emotional discomfort. Quite possibly your husband does as well.

You as a wife cannot deprogram your husband's years of learning to hide insecurity. As Gary put it, "Do you realize how hard it is to work on the foundation of a building? How do you go about rebuilding a whole foundation for security?"

His observation is right. But you can do several things to ease the problem now. One of the best, especially if you have sons, is to keep the problem from affecting the next generation.

First, think about ways you can create as free an atmosphere as possible in your family. Ask yourself, "Do my interactions with my children convey this message: 'I love you if you are well behaved. I love you if you don't cause problems. I love you if show love toward me, which means never expressing anger or frustration. I love you if you are exactly the way I want you to be'?"

Do you see how that is going to breed the kind of conditional love and acceptance that is causing Bubba, Gary, and so many others problems? The pain then spreads to their wives and their marital relationship.

Now think about ways you can convey to your child the message, "I love you! I don't have to put up with tantrums or nasty behavior, but I will acknowledge when you are afraid or angry or sad, and I won't hold that against you. I appreciate good behavior, but I love you any way you are."

Let your son be all that he is, in every dimension—emotional as well as physical. As he grapples with questions regarding personal identity, his purpose in life, and developing relationships, allow him the space to talk and to be, even if he is not what you would wish for him. Even if he talks about uncomfortable things.

In short, parents need to create as free an atmosphere as possible in order to help all children develop fully. This then would allow the growing room to grapple successfully with questions regarding personal identity, purpose in life, and relationship goals. More importantly, the free atmosphere can drive home the message, "You are loved regardless of the ups and downs in your life, regardless of your uncertainties, regardless of your struggles."

Gary wagged his head, incredulous. "I cannot picture Ruthie discussing something like, say, sex with Tiger."

"That then would be something you will talk to him about. If it's a concern of his as he gets older, it's fair game for discussion."

"This is gonna be tough!"

You bet. Too, understand that this atmosphere of freedom is not a cure-all. Kids will still keep certain feelings and curiosities hidden because they are unsure of the reception they would receive were they to reveal all. Doubt is natural. You won't eliminate the problem, but you do well to minimize it.

And now let's explore ways to help your husband move past this dread of having to earn love.

Ruth never knew about the problem of conditional acceptance in Gary's past, and no wonder. Neither of them suspected it, Gary included. That's what counseling is for—to reveal these facets of the self that no one thinks about or suspects.

Also, although it was not Gary's situation, many men who have difficulty being open with their wives feel that their women are judging them even now. They must say the right things and display the right thoughts. In other words, they feel that their wives' love is also conditional.

Know what? They may be right. Examine your own interactions with your husband. Might he, from his point of view, feel that if you think less of him, your love will cool? Have you attached conditions to your affection. "If you would only _____, I'd be more comfortable about loving you."

Only you can reverse that kind of pattern in your relationship, and I strongly urge you to do so! Change your approach both with your actions and also by confessing the past (cite examples if possible; he'll understand better) to him and vowing to love unconditionally in the future.

Now let's assume that you are not attaching conditions to your affection for your man. What next?

When you ease the atmosphere for the kids, you will thereby help ease the problem for your husband as well. He will see, perhaps for the first time, how unconditional love and acceptance look. And he will see that you can offer it.

I asked Gary, "How might Ruth help you move forward from here? How might she ease this feeling that love must be earned by perfection?" *Gary, what can Ruth do so that you can let her see the real house you built rather than the facade?*

One obvious way, of course, was to recognize the price conditional acceptance exacted upon Gary in the past. Simply understanding why a man is the way he is constitutes a big step forward in learning to deal and live with him. Once Ruth could see why Gary behaved as he did, she could be more tolerant.

And consider Lynette. If she could see how Howard's avoiding behavior was based in part on hidden insecurities, she would feel less rejected.

Another help to Gary was for Ruth to accept the prospect that she might be able to provide the safe haven Gary's parents and, indeed, much of the world cannot. Gary might be programmed to conceal his real thoughts and feelings, but he could override that programming with her encouragement.

I might add here that a safe haven means a sealed one. Gary needed the assurance with Ruth that he enjoyed with Bubba. Whatever they discussed, whatever he said, would go no further. A secret forever, no ifs, ands, or buts.

A third was for Ruth to build, and then communicate, her beliefs about the true course of a person's worth. In a hundred subtle ways, Ruth's comments and actions could tell Gary either, "I love you only if you are such-and-so," or else "I love you, and you have immense value." Which of those two messages is most likely to draw a distant husband closer?

## The Fountain of Worth

Gary, Ruth, and I sat in a very early counseling session because Gary had to be on the other side of Dallas in a few hours. Normally, I don't schedule off-hours counsel, but this particular day I had to be out early for other reasons anyway. Besides, Gary was really taking to counseling. Exceedingly reluctant at the beginning, he had warmed to it eagerly.

I opened with, "It's time to talk about the origins of worth. Gary, you and Ruth are both Christians."

Gary nodded. "Ruthie takes to it a little easier'n I do, but yeah. We are."

"And the foundational tenet of the faith?"

Ruth smiled. "Jesus Christ died to save sinners." She then elaborated with a beautiful summary of the gospel. All have sinned and therefore deserve death; Jesus alone did not have the taint of sin. His death on the cross paid for the sins of all others with His own lifeblood. The debt satisfied, He rose again and ascended into heaven.

"So what," I asked, "is the foundation of a person's worth? From what fountains does worth flow?"

Gary, who did not usually appear very introspective, had the answer. "From the fact that God would do all that for me. Hey, you ever hear that old-time gospel hymn, 'There is a Fountain Filled with Blood'?"

"I certainly have heard it. 'I'll sing Thy power to save.'"

"There's your fountain of worth, right there. God thinks I'm worth saving. Can't have a higher compliment than that." Gary sat back, immensely pleased.

"I never suspected you even knew that old song, let alone paid attention to what it meant. Or that you were this spiritual." Ruth turned in her chair to study him. "How come you never once in our marriage talked about deep stuff like this with me?"

"Didn't know you were interested."

"Now," I suggested, "let's recast all this in terms you've been living with all your life, Gary. In fact, you, too, Ruth. For instance,

'Jesus died for me because I hide anger well.' How about, 'Jesus died for me because I support my family'?"

Gary grinned, caught up in the chase. "Okay, let me get this right. You're saying that all the reasons why I have to earn that conditional love we've been talking about aren't any reasons at all. That my worth isn't what other people are saying it is. It's what God says it is."

"Did you earn God's love?"

Ruth jumped in with, "The Bible says He loved us before we even knew Him. And that it's a gift. You can't earn it."

"Right!" Gary was on a roll now. "When you can't earn it, it's the opposite of conditional love, which you have to earn."

"Good!" I led him to the next step. "But we have to move past the intellectual aspect. All that is what we're taught. Now we have to apply it. So let's talk about what difference it might make to know you are valuable to God."

And Gary hesitated. We were now more into the realm of feelings than of head-knowledge, and that was unfamiliar ground to him.

Ruth gave Gary this look of *I know the answer, but I want you to say it,* but Gary didn't notice.

I rephrased it. "If God deems you acceptable in spite of your feelings and mistakes, what effect would that have on your interpretation of conditions placed upon you by men and women?"

"Ah." Gary nodded. "You know, though . . . That would depend on how big I understand God to be. I mean, if God is just a big guy in the sky who sort of oversees the operation but doesn't get involved, then His opinion of me wouldn't weigh very heavy. But if He's big enough to take a personal interest in every human being—me included—then nothing else would matter. This would be a letter of recommendation from the best of the best."

He had the idea. I led him to the conclusion. "Good! Now. In the pattern you've been following so far, you're worried about conditions you have to keep to be acceptable. No anger.

No emotional weakness. No this. No that. When you do that, you're letting others have too much say regarding your worth. You're letting them set the standards, and they are false standards. You learned to do it when you were a boy; either your parents set the standards then or you believed certain standards were necessary."

"I wasn't old enough then to sort out people's standards from God's. As I recall, everything my daddy said might as well have been from God."

I nodded. "That's true of everyone. But now you're an adult. Now you are wise enough to reshape the conditions for acceptance. Now you can ferret out God's standards."

Gary lit up like the national Christmas tree. "But with God there aren't any conditions for acceptance!"

Ruth grumped at him, "Yeah, but I bet if God did have conditions, one of them would be, 'Thou shalt make Tiger go to Sunday school.'"

"No, wait." Gary was staring at me, but I don't think he realized he was doing it. "God loves. Period. But He doesn't necessarily love what we do. The love is unconditional, but our behavior isn't supposed to be. He wants us to live pure lives, but He doesn't base His love on that. We lead pure lives *because* He loves us, not *so that* He loves us!" He wagged his head. "I've been hearing this kind of stuff in church for years, but it never clicked until just now."

"Back to self-esteem, which is where we started. You're letting the opinions of people override God's opinion of you. Do you want to allow that?"

Gary walked out that day a different person, and Ruth for the first time glimpsed the real house Gary had built.

In future sessions we touched on the subject now and then. Gary realized that when he allowed human beings to tell him when he could feel stable, so to speak—in effect usurping God's power—he was standing on shifting sand. That's no security. Once his heart could acknowledge that God alone determines a person's worth, his security was assured, because God's attitude doesn't shift the way people's do.

How do you reach out to your man and show him these truths? I don't know. After all, your presenting problem was his very unwillingness to talk about these deeper things.

I do know one thing that will help immensely in drawing him to you, in leading him to pick the concept up by osmosis to some extent. That one thing is to live the truths Gary discovered, as described above. Let them become your mode of operation. Will he notice? Yes. Will he feel less insecure around you? That's what usually happens. And that in itself will cut the distance.

And it will make you happier. You are loved by God! What a wonderful feeling. Your husband is loved unconditionally by God.

When you live the belief that you do not have to buy acceptance or maintain a prescribed standard, several things will change in your life:

- Defensiveness will abate. When someone points out what he or she perceives to be a flaw, you're no longer afraid to hear it. You need no longer jump to your own defense.
- You don't have to go overboard to impress folks anymore. Being you to the best of your ability is sufficient. That's God's will, not humankind's.
- Relationships will smooth out. As you embrace your own self-acceptance, you'll want others to feel accepted as well.
- Secrets will take far less prominence in your life. If your secret is a true problem—an addiction, a serious fault—correct it. If your secret is a nonproblem to the rest of the world, as so many are, you need no longer spend all that energy keeping it. Either way, your quality of life will improve.
- Selfish thinking patterns will decrease. You will be less consumed by your requirements for emotional and physical comfort. This relaxed attitude can help fretting and performance problems as well.

Understand, I'm not suggesting that walking the walk is easy. Knowing where the fountain of worth really flows and taking full advantage of that knowledge in daily life are two different things.

As Gary put it, "I'll walk out the door in the morning with the best intentions in the world. Then some client will call me on some point, and I'll defend myself without thinking about it. Really get angry because the guy's wrong, and bury it. All the old bad habits. They don't go away when you say 'boo.'"

"Agreed," I replied, "But let's give credit where credit is due here. You're describing a very normal happening. In an unforeseen situation especially, as when a client complains and you weren't expecting it, a person reverts to the reflex reactions. The old habits. You're doing what everyone does, so don't scold yourself. More important, six months ago, you didn't even know you had a problem with self-image and conditional acceptance. Look how far you've come!"

"Yeah, and look how far I have to go. Even at home. Ruthie tries, bless her heart, but she falls back on old habits too. Every now and then she'll cut me down."

"Deliberately?"

"Probably not, but that don't make the cut any shallower. And when she does, I'm getting defensive and thinking, 'Who do you think you are, Sweetheart? The Supreme Court?'"

"Hostile."

"Yeah."

And evasive. The wife then—Ruth, and perhaps you as well—must take extra care that she also is demonstrating acceptance. The old patterns will not go away quickly. They must be banished.

Other patterns of behavior that must be banished are those that erode and exploit trust.

## Trust

Howard Sandstrom put it this way. "Why in the world would I ever spill my heart out to Lynette? She'd go running straight to her pal Kris. You know how girlfriends blab everything. And when she'd get off on one of those what's-wrong-with-old-Howard jags, she'd just use what I said against me. I couldn't win."

Like other aspects involved in burying insecurities, lack of trust can go back to relationships from childhood. Sometimes it is directly tied to major disappointments with other adults. And sometimes it is based directly in the husband-wife relationship.

Repeatedly in my counseling office I talk to men who quite consciously conceal their innermost feelings. Usually, historical lessons have taught them to distrust those who might draw close. For instance, I have heard:

- "No one ever revealed problems in my home because you never knew how severe the punishment was going to be."
- "My older sister was a gossip, and all her friends were gossips. Extended family and school both. I learned real early to avoid telling anything I didn't want spread all over."
- "Maybe I would've talked to someone if I thought they cared, but they seemed preoccupied with other things."
- "My mom was moody. You had to be careful what to say, so I just didn't say anything. I was afraid I'd spark a bad mood."
- "I have no idea what kind of reception I'd get from my wife if I told her, you know, intimate things about me. Or whether her mom would find out all about it an hour later."
- "If anyone brought up those intimate kinds of subjects, and the women were especially good at doing that, we men in the family would hang back and sort of think in unison, 'It's not any of your business!'"

Meanwhile, the wives erroneously interpret this lack of trust as lack of love. "If he loved me, he'd be open and trusting as I am with him." They might even interpret it as sneakiness. "What is this man hiding, that he won't open up?"

Ideally, beginning in infancy, children receive the large doses of attention and nurturing that they need in order to develop well.

Through a proactive approach, parents communicate, "I'm always here for you. You can trust me." As the child grows in awareness and discovers an increasingly complex world out there, the parent's message becomes, "Talk to me. It's safe."

That's the ideal. It's never fully implemented, though many parents come close. When distant husbands like Gary or Howard look back, though, they probably will see that this ideal was not met well at all. They learned to avoid exposing the inner self. It just wasn't safe.

In adulthood, the need for attention and nurturing changes somewhat, but it still exists. Here's the ideal: Friends, marriage partners, and selected coworkers need to project the message, "Please be authentic. You can trust that openness will not be betrayed and it will make your life richer and easier to bear.

I've found it is highly unlikely that if that level of trust was not established, or at least approached, in childhood, that it is unlikely it will be established in adulthood, at least not spontaneously, without a lot of sweat and effort.

Howard, for example, said this in counseling. "I don't ever recall a single conversation with my parents that you would call revealing. That is, revealing inner thoughts and feelings. I see now I could have probably gone to Mom and trusted her to keep it just between us. But Dad was the kind who wanted life to fit in its grooves. He wasn't anywhere near being a touchy-feely type guy, and I see now, looking back, there were two reasons. One is, real men didn't talk about that stuff. His example was burned into me, you might say. And the other is, you don't trust anybody with that kind of thing."

"Vulnerability."

He nodded. "Never make yourself vulnerable deliberately."

"Now you have a problem. You see, a successful marriage requires that there be wide honesty about many personal matters. In due time, Lynette has to be able to see your pitfalls, your insecurities, your anger, your stubbornness, your spirituality or lack of it, your style of love—everything about you. In order to connect successfully with her, you have to lay these matters on the table. Only then can you harmonize who you are with who she is."

Howard sat back, looking stunned as a rabbit that's just been dragged tail first through a drainpipe. "Never in a million years would I have guessed, when I got married, that that's what I'd have to do as a husband. It never occurred to me that I'd have to lay myself open like this."

## Building Trust

Howard and others needed that foundation of trust laid in childhood, if they were to be effective husbands now. You as a wife now know the first thing you have to do. If you are a mother, you want to build that foundation in your children.

Girls must learn trust just as much as boys must, but boys must also be deprogrammed from that concept that they absorb by osmosis, namely, "real men don't discuss such things." Since most boys learn to dismiss this trusting style of communication as a nonessential nuisance, they struggle greatly as husbands when their wives require intimacy and vulnerability. Just as they would act tentatively about approaching a work project with which they had little familiarity, they also can have uncertainties about the foreign, personal dimensions of a marriage relationship.

You earn a child's trust by never ever betraying a confidence and by always allowing the child the right to be heard. This means, in essence, that the child should not hear from you statements such as these:

- "Junior! You know we never talk about those things!"
- "Afraid? That's the silliest thing I ever heard!"
- "Wait until your grandma hears about this!"
- "Your father isn't going to like what you just told me."

See where the trust, fragile at best in a child, would instantly shatter?

In his own practice, a pediatric psychiatrist who is a friend of mine lays these rules at the beginning of his talks with children:

1. You don't have to talk if you don't want to.
2. If you tell me something that directly threatens your life, then and only then will I tell your parents. However, I won't tell them until I have told you I'm doing so, and you can be present when I'm doing it if you wish. (He considers threatening information to be such things as suicidal ideation, weapons in the hands of children, and the use of life-threatening drugs.) Anything else, and I do mean anything, will be held in strictest confidence.
3. Any subject is fair game. Whatever you want to talk about, whatever bothers you.

He never denigrates the child's opinion, ridicules, or dismisses anything. The bond of trust is critical in effective counseling, just as it is critical in an effective marriage. These or similar rules help build it if they are followed faithfully. You might consider establishing rules similar to these with your child and, yes, with your husband as well (deleting the "Tell your parents" part, of course).

As a wife you can take another step toward helping your husband trust. Promote his feelings of security and help him minimize insecurities.

"But isn't that backward?" Lynette protested. "I thought I was supposed to help Howard trust me in order to ease his insecurities, not the other way around."

"It works in both directions. Each feeds on the other," I explained.

The more secure a person feels, the more he does not feel pressed by the weight of conditional acceptance, the easier it will be for him to trust. The easier it is to trust, the more his insecurities will ease. A lack of trust in others often denotes a lack of trust in the self—that old "Do I measure up?" doubt.

Paradoxically, the most secure man is the one who openly admits that he doesn't always have his act together. You as a wife already know about some of those insecurities, at least in part. Because you do, he will not lose face as he becomes more open, and, indeed, he will gain a solid measure of credibility. You can probably impart that truth to him by actions more so than words.

A friend of mine often repeats the down-home saying, "Love me, love my dog." He has expanded it far beyond dogs. He means, "When you attach to me, you also get whatever is part of me." It is so much simpler to be able to reveal the whole than to cut the self up into segments. "Let the world see this one, conceal that one, let a few see this, let that be buried forever."

You the wife can take the lead here, approaching anything he might reveal about himself with respect. This isn't easy for him. This is proprietary information he's letting see the light of day. The woman who appreciates that a man has much more difficulty talking of intimate things than does she, and imparts that appreciation however she can, will do much for her husband.

Don't discount the value of counseling here. Oftentimes, a disinterested third party can help the bond of trust develop more quickly by guiding it. That third party is "safe" and can show both husband and wife what trust entails and how to achieve it. Results occur more quickly with less chance of a backfire—a misplacement of trust.

Most men would love to be able to trust. They could do it if only they hadn't been so thoroughly trained to mistrust. Leading a man to that level of intimacy improves his life every bit as much as it improves the life of the woman who wants the deeper relationship.

## The Goals

Performance-oriented people appreciate goals. And unburdening the self of those buried insecurities, the primary goal, achieves these secondary goals. The husband and wife have somewhat differing goals, which I'll label His and Hers:

- His: No longer as defensive, the husband becomes less concerned about being dogmatically correct and more concerned about hearing what his wife is actually saying. You'll recall that's been one of her goals all along.

- Hers: When he fails to meet his goal above, she need not feel immediately rejected. He's not rejecting her per se.
- His: When she brings up a problem, he's less likely to get into trouble if he doesn't respond the way she thinks he should have. Awareness that wrath is not going to descend upon him frees him to actually be more open and less guarded.
- Hers: The world no longer ends if she brings up a problem or topic and he doesn't follow her script.
- His: He can say, "I need help" when he needs help.
- Hers: She can help him productively when he needs it.
- Both: When either feels moody or stressed, the other understands and does not take it personally. Neither need keep up a facade.

And one other great good comes of this. The wife no longer feels, "Why does he treat me this way?" Whether he alters his habits or not, she now knows why. The problem is not all him. It's his past as well. Some of the problem is you. Nothing's perfect, but now you know how to minimize imperfection.

Although we discussed for a full chapter the man's hidden insecurities, I do not mean to suggest the wife has none. She has her own set of insecurities to manage. When she can learn to operate from a position of inner strength and stability, putting those insecurities in their place, her communications will be more fruitful. And that's the subject of the next chapter.

*chapter 8*

# $\mathcal{H}$er Self-Image Struggles

*O*nce upon a time, Jean Moreland made people laugh. She looked and acted like the stereotype of a librarian: petite, dark-haired, unassuming, and quiet. In a room full of people, she would be nearly the last one you'd notice. Then she would say something warm and funny that set the people she was talking to giggling. She would move to a new group and laughter would break out there. Before long, although no one realized what was happening, her sweet, gentle humor had brightened the mood of the whole room. When people suggested she try stand-up comedy or humor writing, she simply smiled. No, she couldn't do that, performing before crowds either live or in print.

Jean Moreland didn't make people laugh anymore. She rarely appeared in public and never accepted invitations. On those occasions when she absolutely had to join her husband, Mark, at some social function, she stood around "like a gatepost," as he put it.

She showed up in my office, not at Mark's insistence but at a friend's. The friend, Lonnie, provided transportation and waited in the clinic reception area. "I'm guarding the door so Jean doesn't split," claimed Lonnie. Jean was, to say the least, reluctant to seek counsel.

"Lonnie's overstating things," Jean insisted to me. "She says I have all the classic symptoms of depression. But I don't have anything to be depressed about, so it's just a mood swing."

"Symptoms such as . . . ?" I asked.

She shrugged. "Sleep patterns are what worried Lonnie. I fall asleep okay, but I wake up around two in the morning and can't go back. And appetite, I have no appetite. Sometimes I have stomach problems."

"Sexual interest?"

Those frail shoulders bobbed again. "So-so. About average, I suppose, for someone married twelve years."

It turned out not to be average at all. Her interest in sexual involvement had nose-dived at about the same time as her spirits. As we talked, Jean appeared to be showing signs of major burnout, so I began digging for possible stress causes.

Work? She sent the kids off to school and worked mornings as a hospital receptionist. She described her work as "going along about as always. The usual bin of loonies, fun to work with. Medical personnel have this really warped sense of humor. But I guess you know that."

Kids? "Three, all doing fine. Austin (the oldest, age ten) gets into trouble occasionally, but nothing serious. He's just all boy. Really active. Maybe hyperactive but not enough to affect grades or anything."

Extended family? Was there any illness, marital problems, or the like occurring to relatives, especially well-loved relatives? No. "Usual ups and downs, but nothing drastic."

Money? "Mark makes a very good living as a computer specialist with a phone company, and I am well paid as receptionists go. No problems with money."

Marriage? "Not very good, but that's not news."

Bingo.

Jean failed to see her marriage as a source of stress because she couldn't identify any significant change lately. It never had been doing well. She did not feel emotionally close to Mark anymore, in part because he worked long hours but mostly because he spent most of his free time at home hacking, as she called it. Late into the night, he'd be sitting at his computer in the fourth bedroom, which he had converted into a den. Call it a lair. The kids were forbidden to enter, and Jean felt like a trespasser when she went in periodically to clean.

Mark took very little interest in Jean or her pursuits. If he had any expectations for her as a wife beyond the sexual aspect, he never voiced them.

Jean summarized it well. "I sometimes wonder why Mark even bothers being married. What's the point? He could hire someone to do for him what I do." She turned a bit red. "I don't mean the sex, of course. You know what I mean. But then, lately he hasn't been asking for very much of that."

When I asked specifically how far back her concerns about her marriage extended, she replied, "I guess not until four or five years into it. You know how when you're young and just starting, you kind of grope your way through life. He was constantly agitated about something or other, and I was a bundle of nerves. I had a really stressful job then too. When Austin came, and then the girls, he seemed to withdraw more and more. So it's been building."

"How about the last six months? Anything deteriorated markedly in the last six months?"

She turned to ice.

I waited.

Her voice vibrated with quiet fury. "Mark is into porn."

"And you found out about it around the time these symptoms of depression began."

"Yes."

## ☙ *THE BEATING A SELF-IMAGE TAKES*

Six months ago, their son got into a huge argument with his dad when Mark, suspecting something, opened a package delivered in Austin's name. The parcel was relatively innocuous: some CDs. But Austin, furious, opened one of his dad's incoming packages in retaliation and found a videotape.

Jean recalled, "Austin tried to hide it, of course, but I was in the next room when he opened it, and I heard him gasp. I took it away from him and confronted Mark that night. He was enraged at Austin, of course. That's expected. But he was enraged at me too. To say that was unexpected is understating it. Here he is, wrapped up in just plain sin, and he began yelling at me, as if I were the guilty party. I actually believe he thinks I am! He's laid it all on me!"

I explained about the psychological concept of projection, wherein a person projects his or her own faults and dislikes onto another person. We talked a few more minutes. Then she broke up completely.

Sobbing, she roared, "He's a church member! He's supposed to know right from wrong! It's not even soft porn! What's wrong with me that he needs that stuff! Why couldn't I hold on to him?"

## The Deep Sources of a Woman's Insecurity

Do you hear the death of Jean's self-image in her voice? One of the most primal of needs, not just to be loved but to be loved by your mate, is often made the wife's responsibility, whether it ought to be or not. When society rates a woman, sex appeal weighs heavily. Unfortunate, but that's the way it is. In her own eyes, Jean had flunked one of our culture's most basic tests, though in actuality, she had not.

And do you see how Jean was experiencing the doubts and emotions so common to women with evasive, distant husbands? He might be the one with a multitude of hang-ups and imbalances, yet she assumed it implied that there was something fundamentally wrong with her.

As a very general rule with many exceptions, women have what is called a nesting instinct. It is the reason they take great pride and pleasure in creating a warm, cozy home atmosphere that keeps the family feeling vibrant. These women see it as their role to be the strong support system that enables the family members to feel secure and loved. When the home is a positive, intact place, these women feel good about themselves, secure in the fact that they are serving their purpose. When something goes haywire in the nest, so to speak, their feelings of self-worth plummet.

But what happens when the husband decides he's not interested in what she contributes? That's his decision, and he's a responsible adult. She feels it's her fault anyway. If only she had [fill in the blank]. Self-doubt congeals into self-loathing.

"Would you believe a friend of mine at church is a private detective?" Jean smiled sadly. "No one ever meets a private detective, let alone knows one. Stuff of fiction. But she is one. Almost all her work, she says, is simply researching records. No guns, no daring stuff. Rarely a stakeout. Anyway, after I found out about Mark's, uh, obsession, I asked her to look into it, see how deeply he was involved. I mean, it might have been the only tape he ever bought, right?"

"Did you feel you were invading Mark's privacy?"

"Yes, and that's crazy. He's my husband. Of one flesh. So I took a day off from work, and Laurel came over one morning after the kids and Mark went out. To use her phrase, she tossed the den. That is, she searched it. He has a library of dozens of pornographic videos behind some old boxes of junk in the closet. Then she did some hacking on his computer. He has a separate charge account for his computer hours so they don't show up on our joint card. She obtained records of his video rentals, his internet hours, even some of his book and magazine purchases . . . I was staggered. Stunned."

"By the extent of it."

Jean nodded. "Know what? Laurel just sat and hugged me

while I cried. How many private detectives in the mystery novels do that for you?"

"Jean, you had no inkling of this previously? We're looking for additional stress sources here."

"My imagination really geared up, once this came out in the open. I started remembering all the excuses he gave me for not being home. He'd work late. A friend would call with tickets to the ball game. He'd stop at his mom's. Take a client to dinner. He always had some reason to spend time with anyone but me."

"Did you confront him about any of this prior to six months ago?"

"A few times."

"How did he respond?"

"I'd tell him how much I need a marriage partner who actually wants to be with me, and I always got the same response. He'd become irate and sarcastic, then go bury himself in his den. I decided the confrontation wasn't worth it and just made him more distant. I realize now I was the classic enabler. Buried my head in the sand."

What were the mechanics of this situation? Where were Jean Moreland's symptoms of depression coming from? In large measure, they were a direct result of handing over her emotional stability to someone who was either unwilling or unable to keep her feeling good about herself. The depression was a product of building her self-esteem upon her husband's attitude and his treatment of her. Need I point out that no woman can control a man's attitudes?

## How Is Your Self-Image?

Have you ever had similar problems? Have you ever wondered if the behavior and attitudes your husband expresses indicate that you're just not making the grade as a wife? If so, you are susceptible, as was Jean, to getting caught in an uncontrollable situation that will create all sorts of doubt regarding your status as a woman who deserves the highest regard.

In order to draw the distant husband closer rather than furthering his evasiveness, you must unhook yourself emotionally from his behavior. You will need to seize the truth that your security and value do not rise or fall based upon his feelings of the moment toward you. Yes, your quality of life may suffer because of his uncooperative ways, but your self-esteem does not have to fly out the window as well. His problems, whatever they are, do not have to dictate your self-image. They need not damage your belief in yourself.

In order to prevent that from happening, it helps very much to know just how vulnerable you are to the problem of shaky self-esteem. To evaluate your vulnerability, check the statements that apply to you:

_____ 1. As I think about it, I will consistently suppress discussing my own needs and allow my husband's to take top priority.

_____ 2. When I do complain or vent frustrations, my problems don't seem to matter to him.

_____ 3. I used to be cheerier and more optimistic than I am now.

_____ 4. My head knows my husband's problems would exist regardless of whether I were here or not, but my heart keeps wondering what I did to cause him to be the way he is.

_____ 5. I'm beginning to wonder if perhaps I'm expecting too much, that my perceived needs are excessive.

_____ 6. I feel that I have to prove to myself that I'm okay. I have standards and expectations to meet.

_____ 7. Lately, I find myself more frequently in a discouraged or edgy mood.

_____ 8. When I think about the future, I worry that I can't handle the challenges that lie ahead.

_____ 9. Instead of just mentioning or stating preferences, I find myself pleading and begging.

_____ 10. I can frequently catch myself in self-doubt: Am I appealing? Did I do something wrong? Am I inadequate?

_____ 11. When I talk with friends or extended family, I'm more pessimistic and cynical than I was in the past.

_____ 12. I compare myself negatively with other women who seem to have it together.

No doubt you checked a few items, or at least thought about checking them. No one feels secure about herself all the time. Doubts assail even so-called "perfect" women and even women with nannies and secretaries and butlers to take some of the load. However, if you feel six or more items are describing you, you probably ought to work at rooting out some insecurities with which you struggle. I might also add, you're probably being too hard on yourself.

Let's consider Jean Moreland's situation. She fell into the common temptation: she focused her energies almost wholly upon her marriage. More specifically, she was consumed by this problem: "Mark's behavior is unacceptable, particularly for a married man and most particularly for a man married to me. What will it take for me to shape him up?" You can see, I'm sure, how she was setting herself up for bitter, bitter disappointment.

She was caught up in another tricky trap as well. She was centering her whole self-image upon her marriage. She was letting Mark's inability to provide adequate love, or perhaps simply his neglect to provide it, destroy her confidence in herself.

Lynette was doing that with Howard as well, at least to some extent. Lynette, of course, did not face the severe problem that Mark's pornography addiction forced upon Jean. Still, Lynette habitually pressed for Howard to make her feel good about herself, virtually guaranteeing that he would move farther from her.

Ideally, Jean and I both agreed, Mark would take it upon himself to buoy her self-esteem. After all, that is a major function of marriage. But in the event that he did not, she needed enough staying power to remain confident in herself. Too, like most women in this situation, Jean did not have to shamefully assume she was an inadequate woman.

I led both of these women to become aware of the three ten-dencies that often shape a woman's struggle with self-image: lack of an emotional fallback position, an emphasis on external, super-ficial qualities when forming self-esteem, and a lack of decisive-ness when it comes to managing emotions.

## Lack of an Emotional Fallback Position

As I got to know Jean on a deeper psychological level, I real-ized that she had long been predisposed to letting her self-image be dictated by outside forces. That came home powerfully as she talked about her mother, Grace, now in her late sixties.

"Mom? The sweetest woman you'd ever hope to know. She never complained, and Dad wasn't often very sweet toward her. She worked constantly for us, more a servant than a family mem-ber. She was always willing and available if we wanted something. She was even available for our school friends. Just a terrific mom!"

"And your father indicated his approval of her?"

"I don't think so. I never saw it."

"Did he openly display pleasure in her service toward him and his children?"

"Well, no. There was this understanding, you see. He'd sup-port the family, and she'd attend to her duties. An assumption. I don't remember that either one of them gave each other any pos-itive reinforcement. I mean, encouragement."

As Jean grew, she learned that mind-set. Do what you're sup-posed to. Keep up the good grades. Be sweet. Don't complain. Don't make waves. During her college years, her horizons expanded considerably. She saw that if she would make her own way, she would have to be more assertive, make a few waves, complain when complaint was appropriate.

But when she married, the old habits took over. Her mother had modeled a particular style that she adopted without realizing it. Mark didn't help; he considered any woman with a mind of her own to be "uppity," and he let his opinion be known.

Jean didn't always cave in. She made her feelings and needs known, often quite forcefully. However, when Mark responded unfavorably, she would sometimes come unhinged. Then he'd lecture her on the folly of being a wimpy woman who expected her husband to take care of everything for her with no effort on her own part.

If you see an inconsistency here on Mark's part—speaking badly of both independent women and clinging vines—you're right. Almost never are marital disagreements based on logic.

What do you think? Because of that inconsistency, in essence, Mark was telling his wife not to have any needs or expectations. Was he on target? Should Jean have learned to be satisfied separate from him?

As I have worked with many couples through the years, I have come to hold some pessimistic beliefs. Perhaps they're not so much pessimistic as pragmatic, but they're not rosy. I believe Jean should indeed seek sources for self-image and security beyond her marriage and husband. Jean's expectations that Mark help fulfill her own life and needs were not unreasonable at all. My pessimism, though, tells me that while God's design for marriage was intended as a place to have many needs met, people like Mark show no regard for that design. Simply put, the design is still excellent, but too often the people entrusted to live out that design are flawed to a degree that the partner, frustrated, will remain unfulfilled.

Jean needed a fallback plan. Perhaps you do too.

I asked Jean, "When you were growing up, what kind of preparation did you receive for the possibility of disappointment in love?"

She stared. "What kind of question is that?"

"Love is never perfect. Everyone is disappointed to some extent. How did your parents train you to deal with that certainty of disappointment?"

"Well, uh . . ." She shrugged. "None, I guess. All the talks about relationships were between Mom and me. She preached a great deal about maintaining the right morals and values, and she emphasized how I had to pick a man who shared those values. But not . . . uh, you know, getting over a loused-up love."

"I'm not being critical. It's important that your mother would give you such guidance. But listen for a moment to the unspoken message in what you just said. 'Pick a man who shares those values.' The implied message is, 'You'll find security when a man gives you the right ingredients.'"

"You're saying it was wrong for her to teach me that?"

"No. It's true that you can find peace and security when a man loves and nurtures you. And matching his moral values to yours is extremely important. But here's the catch: as a young woman you were idealistic enough to believe that your man would eagerly want to serve in that support role. You had no safety net in place to catch you if he failed the role."

"What kind of safety net?"

"You've been talking about moral values, church, and God, and mentioned that Mark is also a church member. This is going to sound like a cliché, something you've heard many times. Your backup is actually what you could call your front-up. Your ultimate identity and security rests safely in God. He, not Mark, is the author of inner security."

In the previous chapter, we talked about how a man must build his image and confidence based upon God's opinion of him, not humankind's. It is equally true for the wife.

How deeply have you considered your importance in the eyes of God? Do you understand that human rejection and insensitivity do not veto the value the Creator Himself has bestowed upon you? If so, what difference does it make?

Jean figured it out. "When I lose sight of my standing before God, I substitute Mark's opinion of me. But he doesn't want to be there for me. He doesn't even know how. I've been setting myself up for guaranteed failure."

Can you say the same about your situation?

Here is the path Jean followed in developing a fallback

position. I suggest that as you go through her steps, you adapt them to the particulars of your own relationship.

- Jean recognized that Mark's opinions, or lack of them, did not determine her worth and did not shape her image.
- It was counterproductive for her to assume that sooner or later he would agree with God. Indeed, he was severely out of touch with God. She would therefore keep her eyes on the real measure of her worth.
- She would act in Mark's best interests, of course, but she need not nag and plead and throw fits, which amounted to empty communication. She had a duty to identify what she saw as right and wrong, but it was beyond her ability to force Mark in some way. He was an adult who must make his own decisions.

Jean would find that the hardest part of adjusting her thinking here would stem from the frustration that Mark quite probably would never fully agree with her self-assessment. For one thing, he hardly ever thought about lofty subjects such as godly worth, and for another, he had lapsed into a habit of seeing her only from a critical, insensitive point of view. He had ceased to see the good in her. That was very hard to take.

She wagged her head. "All right, so what do I do next?"

"I suggest learning to practice what I call *delicate detachment.* By that I mean that you can separate your thinking from his when you know his thoughts are off base, but you can do it gently."

"Not coming unglued."

"More than that. Not just on the outside. On the inside as well. It requires immense discipline, which takes practice, but once you come to terms with the fact that Mark cannot have ultimate power over your self-esteem unless you give it to him, you'll find yourself making progress."

She sighed. "Obviously, this isn't going to come easily, let alone automatically. But I can't go on the way I have been."

"Keep in mind," I continued, "that this doesn't mean you ought never to confront or tell him what you want. You owe it to yourself and to him to be honest about what you want and what you are. I'm saying that your belief in your own worthiness is the safety net to sustain you at those times when he doesn't adequately respond."

We discussed the influences that external forces exert as well.

## Emphasis on External, Superficial Qualities

Jean Moreland seemed far more relaxed on her next visit. She said, "It's refreshing and stimulating to discuss a spiritually grounded self-image. So many times, I heard people talk about the need for an inner guidance system, but I never really knew what it meant."

"Sometimes you have to reach a breakdown point before you're ready to face issues like that. I think it's excellent that you're taking a negative situation . . ."

"Mark's problems and his inability to relate to me well."

"Yes. And you're turning it into a positive situation—rebuilding your stability from the inside out. Tell me. As you were growing up, just what *did* you build your self-esteem around?"

"Easy question. Good grades. In elementary and high school both, I was supposed to be the kid with the good grades."

"So you could feel acceptable as long as you were making A's and B's?"

"No B's allowed. My dad really emphasized how proud he was when I brought home all A's. But grades weren't all. Popularity too. In high school I was on the drill team and ran cross-country. Hung out with the most popular guys. I saw the girls who didn't click with the right people and how it affected them negatively. There was no way I was going to be left out."

Before we negatively jump onto this information about Jean's past, information so many, many women share, let's ask: Was it wrong or ill-advised for her to draw her self-esteem from achievement and popularity? Think about the social atmosphere in your formative years. Do you recall how security and confidence came to the ones who had the advantage in these areas?

It's very natural for girls, and boys as well, to find their self-esteem in achievement and social acceptance. They aren't adult enough yet to incorporate abstract notions that will eventually become the foundation of self-esteem, as could Jean in her maturity. They need those concrete measurements. Jean's history paralleled most women's.

Each developing person, though, must eventually learn the balance regarding the importance of superficial elements of self-esteem versus the more abstract elements. This is where many adults should look back to discover where shortages lie.

And here's where our childhoods so often play a dastardly trick. Our early training too often diligently prepares us for the wrong attitude.

Look at your own background. You were taught to dress attractively and have the right hairstyle, but were you also encouraged to live anchored in your inner beauty? Perhaps you felt pressed to become socially adept, even coy with the boys, but were you also challenged to communicate authentically and with openness? Surely you learned the importance of projecting a cheerful and friendly demeanor, but how often were you stimulated to know the meaning of your anger and how to successfully negotiate conflicts? Ideally, your identity is wrapped up in much more than the external, superficial qualities, but if you are like many adult women, you may recall little training in the loftier abstracts that truly matter.

"It was all of society teaching externals, not just family." Jean recalled, "I can remember how embarrassed I would be in college if I had to be seen in public without makeup. A fire drill in the dorm at 2 A.M.? Grab your lipstick on the way out. And you had to be picture perfect if any guys were around. Don't let anyone know you don't look perfect. That stuff is laughable now, but at the time, your identity, your very life, and world peace hung on appearing exactly right."

Far too often, the husbands don't help a bit. Many times I've listened to men in counseling complain about the emphasis women place upon trivia such as wearing perfectly color-coordinated clothes or greeting acquaintances correctly in public. Of course, they too often hinge their own image upon possessing the perfect-looking wife. I adjure you to give these minor matters the attention due them, which is not much at all, and hinge your image and your security upon something real.

Jean learned to overcome the disappointments that arose from her less-than-satisfying marriage by anchoring herself in these less trivial things. She enjoyed the challenge, she once claimed, of shifting her focus away from looks and popularity. "I know," she said, "that this shift doesn't really change anything on the outside, especially Mark. But it makes it all so much easier to live with."

## Lack of Planning Emotions

"Plan emotions? You can't be serious!" Jean wagged her head.

"Not exactly plan as much as to choose strategies in advance."

"That still doesn't sound like it would work." She thought about it a moment. "Of course, I have to admit that right now, my emotions just sort of happen. Something occurs, and I react. Sometimes my reaction makes matters worse. Are you saying that's what I can plan better?"

"Exactly."

How often has your husband tossed cold water on a discussion by commenting:

- "Don't get so worked up. Good grief."
- "Why are you always so uptight?"
- "Quit making such a big deal out of it."
- "I didn't mean to make you cry, but why are you getting so upset?"
- "I don't know what to do when you fall apart like this."

Allowing your emotions to carry you away damages your ability to be persuasive. But notice especially the implied message when your emotions go up and down with the circumstances. It says that you are unable to maintain personal stability unless the person or situation in question goes your way. That's certainly not the message of powerlessness that you want to convey.

What if Mark fails to repent of his addiction? What if Howard refuses to engage Lynette in any conversation deeper than about the weather? What if Gary continues to let Ruth make all the significant parenting decisions? Does that doom their women to a life of insecurity and shaky self-image? Women with distant, evasive husbands often work themselves into a state of instability because they mistakenly assume their value, their image as women and wives, is inexorably tied to their husbands. This instability often evidences itself on the surface as a lack of calm.

All right, let's assume these husbands are uncooperative in their relationships. They're not going to make the effort to help their women feel good (and in all fairness, I point out it is probably because they cannot understand what's needed). The wife must take back the power to make her happy that she handed over to her man. She has to wrench back into her own hands the responsibility for her feelings.

Jean shook her head. "It doesn't work that way! I can't help myself. I uncork before I can grab my emotions, if you want to say it that way. And especially when Mark tells me what I'm supposed to be feeling. That infuriates me instantly! He's not only telling me that my emotions are not what he thinks they should be, he's telling me what they ought to be!"

Many wives can relate to her statement there.

Think back to your own childhood. How were your feelings addressed? Some girls, like most boys, learned early to quell external signs of emotion because it was not safe to expose them. One or both parents might have been rigid about refusing "unseemly" emotional expression.

But most women recall that they were allowed a fairly broad range of emotional expression, usually far more than boys. Girls can cry. Girls can come apart. In a sense it is expected: adolescent girls in particular are usually considered volatile.

I asked Jean specifically, "What reception did you get when you let your feelings have free play?"

"If I was angry—especially if I was loud and angry—I was reprimanded. Girls don't voice anger that way. But when I was hurt, discouraged—happy, for that matter—Mother in particular was willing to let me go. She was a better-than-average listener too. Remember? I told you how sweet she was."

"In what ways did she encourage you to search for the purpose behind your feelings? How did she teach you to keep your feelings from going too far to an extreme?"

"Huh?"

Jean is not alone. It is helpful and necessary that parents soothe their children as they experience powerful emotions. This attention and comfort makes the child feel safe and accepted. But soothing and listening do not complete the child's need. Beyond that, the child needs encouragement to explore why the emotion is there, to understand what is healthy about it, and to take responsibility for its direction when it gains too powerful a hold. Hardly ever do they receive that.

The child enters adulthood still looking to those around her for the soothing and comfort she needs, just as she did as a child. It never occurs to her to take over that responsibility, although she assumes the other, more obvious, adult responsibilities. She didn't realize it was there. This looking to the outside instead of within proves disastrous when the person she looks to is an evasive or distant man.

Planning in Jean's case would consist of two things: working out in advance where her self-image is going to come from and working out in advance now she is going to respond to the man she married. Attending to those two details will help her immensely in keeping emotions in the realm in which they ought to remain.

## Seeking Alternatives

On one occasion, I asked Jean to write down a list of times when her sense of security and her self-image were damaged by actions Mark took. They could be solitary events or patterns of behavior. Here is a sampling from her rather lengthy list:

- He makes negative comments about my body, and he can spot a beautiful woman a mile away.
- There was this new film I really wanted to see. When I asked him to take me, he said he had other plans. Know what they were? Watching a ball game on TV.
- When I tell him about some concern, just about any concern, he doesn't take me seriously. I even told him about a leak behind the shower stall, and he didn't believe me until a visiting male friend who used the bathroom told him about it.
- He ignores me in public.
- We always have sex his way.
- He was on the Internet again, seeking out titillation.

What would happen if Jean took that list to Mark? I can pretty safely predict that he would say, "These things are nothing more than harmless, minor irritations, if that. You're too sensitive." That is Mark's way of saying, "I don't want to take the trouble to try to change. You're on your own with your emotional bungee cord." In short, Mark would disavow responsibility. I say that because many husbands do the same.

With Mark unwilling to do so, Jean herself would have to take on the responsibility to shape her image and control her emotions. She actively decided to do so when she took a good look at that list and realized the control Mark, with his irresponsibility, wielded over her inner person.

What if you were to make a list? You could do one of two things with it. If you dwelt upon it, your slipping feelings of adequacy would plummet further. But if you analyzed it, you would see that these opinions expressed in word and deed do not reflect the opinion in which God holds you—indeed, in which most of your friends hold you. That list could be your wake-up call to take charge.

How do you take charge? How do you plan emotional

responses and choose alternatives to the way things have been going?

By illustration, let's see how Jean handled one occasion.

I asked her to pick an event coming up in which she was likely to feel snubbed or belittled, and decide in advance how a fully confident Jean (or, if she can't picture that, a fully confident other woman) would handle it.

She thought a moment. "Tomorrow evening we're going over to his parents' house. His parents don't like kids much, even their grandchildren, so we're getting a sitter. Is that weird, or what?"

It said something about how Mark was raised.

She continued, "Talk about aloof. Mark and his dad play remote roulette in front of the TV, and his mom and I do the dishes. She wants her kitchen cleaned up before we leave, she says, and you can guess why. During dinner, Mark won't pay any attention to me, and after dinner it is going to be worse. If he sees some chick on television, he'll compare me to her unfavorably."

"I hear a pattern here."

"You sure do."

In order to allow light at the end of the tunnel, we set a time constraint—from 7 to 10 P.M. For three hours she would:

- Actively watch out for put-downs and snubs.
- Consider their source and with self-talk remind herself that this was not an accurate picture of herself. This was a view seen through a warped screen—her husband's inaccurate opinions.
- She would focus on her true measures of worth—God's opinion, the words of trusted friends who knew her, and the kind of confidence in her own abilities a secure woman would enjoy.

In her case, I suggested one other step that she normally takes in social groupings though, apparently, hardly ever with her husband and in-laws—her legendary gentle humor.

"It's no use," she said. "They wouldn't appreciate it."

"No, but you would."

She smiled. "Entertain myself, if no one else. I get the absurdity and humor even if they don't. I like it."

Can you do that? Take responsibility for your personal image regardless your husband's behavior? Claim your own solid goals?

The key ingredient is to hang on to your own inner steering wheel.

Now let's get to the crux of marriage: building stronger relationship skills.

*chapter 9*

# *F*ive Keys to Successful Relating

*L*et's call him John.

John's life was going down the tubes.

His body was deteriorating. He worked out three days a week, sometimes four, but he was getting a potbelly anyway. He had his hair touched up and styled, but he still looked his fifty-four years—at least fifty-four. And he was starting to feel pretty stiff and creaky at times.

His job was deteriorating. At the pharmaceutical corporation where he worked in upper management, they had recently bumped him upstairs to a largely ceremonial position—in fact, it was actually a demotion. "I can see the writing on the wall," he claimed. "Early retirement whether I want it or not, and the golden parachute's gonna be brass."

His home life had long since deteriorated. His first wife, after a lengthy affair ("Sometimes I'm a little slow to smell the coffee," he mused), divorced him, and he had seen their two children only sporadically since. He remarried, and now his present wife of eighteen years was making noises about leaving him. Their eleven-year-old son had twice been suspended for threatening his teacher, and their almost-sixteen-year-old daughter was sexually involved with a twenty-year-old college student.

His house needed a new roof, his car had a brake problem that mechanics claimed they couldn't find, and this morning he accidentally ran over his expensive cellular phone.

He waved a hand airily. "So go ahead, Doc. Tell me the Internal Revenue Service is fingering me for an audit. It's the only thing left."

"So you're chin-deep in problems and no end in sight."

"Don't tell me." And then he turned serious. "When Beverly announced she was going to walk, my first thought was, 'Good riddance. If you can't tell when you have a sweet deal, good-bye.' But then when I was playing racquetball the next day, my heart got a funny thing going. Panicked me! I ended up in the hospital overnight while they strapped one of those monitors to my chest. Next day they did the whole treadmill thing. Know what the cardiologist says? I got a seventy-year-old heart in a forty-year-old body. He says that averages out to about my age, but it sure isn't good."

I let him talk. That's often the major part of counseling.

He continued. "Lying in a hospital bed, no phone calls, no work, no visitors, what's left? I had to think. Couldn't sleep. You got a box belted to your chest listening to your heart tick wrong, you don't sleep. Trust me on that. Beverly said I hadn't done a solitary thing to make our marriage work. I tried to think of something, just to prove her wrong. I couldn't. I've done absolutely zip to support my marriage. And I'll do you one worse. I can't think of a single thing I did to save my first one, either." Almost as an afterthought, he added sorrowfully, "My first two kids hardly speak to me. What's wrong with this picture?"

I know soul-searching when I see it. This man was on the cusp of some pretty good insights. I asked, "What do *you* think is wrong, John?"

"Me. That's what's wrong, plain and simple. My life is so

screwed up. Until now, I blamed one screwup on this person and that screwup on that person. But there's too many of them. Those were good women I married. The kids started out good. Everything started out good. It's got to be me."

His Beverly had laid out in no uncertain terms how serious their problem was, and perhaps for the first time in his life, John was listening. In no way was I going to detract from that awareness with a reassuring, "Now, John, don't be so hard on yourself." He needed this agonizing self-appraisal, and I wanted to be there to help put the wheels into motion to make something good come from his open admission.

I suppose the most refreshing experience for me as a psychotherapist comes when a person admits with no finger-pointing, with no justification or excuses, "I want help, and I'm not quitting until my life is drastically better." That's where John was, and I was pulling for him!

In our subsequent sessions, John and I zeroed in on many of the ideas discussed in early chapters of this book. He was a classic, textbook, type A, performance-oriented go-getter. While he was not the raging sort of husband, he displayed anger frequently and often, we decided, used it as "a tool to keep Beverly and the kids in line" (his words). He was impatient with Beverly's feminine outlook on things, showed all the signs of a control freak, admitted eventually to powerful insecurities—you name it, he was there.

As each session passed, John became more and more convinced that he must set aside some of the qualities he cherished most because, bottom line, they made him an unfit spouse and father. He actively sought the necessary adjustments that would lead to a richer personal life. And regularly, I complimented and encouraged his efforts.

## HUSBAND AND WIFE TOGETHER

Let us make a few assumptions here. Let's assume that one way or another, one spouse convinces the other that changes must be made, and they agree, at least tentatively, to make those changes jointly. One or the other may approach the task tentatively, even reluctantly, but the two of you, having committed to marriage, are now going to commit to making it work.

Should one or the other refuse to take that step, you can still make progress. We'll discuss that situation in the next chapter.

You may be, like John or like Keith Troy, the man with the anger problem, a spouse who has decided you can no longer avoid the effort required to harmonize two very different personalities. Perhaps like Ruth, Lynette, or Beverly, you choose not to sit by idly and watch a potentially good relationship go down the tubes.

Whichever angle you may be coming from, it would be a good idea at this point to do a quick self-appraisal. The following items can help you discern if you are really ready to make the adjustments needed in your home life. Which ones apply strongly to you? Be honest as you respond!

_____ 1. Whatever mistakes I have made in my marriage, I cannot justify them by claiming they were someone else's fault. My own choices helped get me where I am.

_____ 2. I accept (I'm tempted to say "welcome" here) accountability from people who know that I have plenty of ways I could improve as a spouse.

_____ 3. When I believe someone is wrong in their critical assessment of me, I nonetheless accept that there are some useful nuggets there for me to mine.

_____ 4. You bet I can be stubborn! Perhaps it's time to temper that stubbornness.

_____ 5. My spouse has legitimate wants and needs that I can no longer afford to ignore.

_____ 6. I believe in the Golden Rule: Do unto others as you would have them do unto you.

_____ 7. When I'm standing up for my needs, I'd get farther and do better if I would also consider the needs of other persons in my life.

_____ 8. When my mate lets down emotionally, that's no excuse for me to do the same.

_____ 9. I believe future successes need not be doomed by past mistakes.

_____ 10. Saying, "That's just the way I am," is a lazy cop-out. I can change.

_____ 11. Relationships deserve first priority in my life. My marriage will receive my best efforts.

_____ 12. I believe that the ability to love is ultimately determined by choice, not frilly feelings.

Each of these statements represents a key idea necessary for relational growth. In order to make the appropriate adjustments, it would be most helpful if you could respond affirmatively to as many of them as possible. Look back over those you did not check and consider why you could not. Be willing to directly confront your beliefs in a way that will keep you looking forward.

I suggested to John, "Let's put our heads together and figure out what a good, healthy style of relating consists of and how to achieve it."

When I work with people like John and Beverly, Howard and Lynette, and Ruth and Gary, I try to help them incorporate into their everyday lives certain ideas that can do much to promote relational success. One deals with time.

## Time Is a Front-Line Priority

Say all you want about changing attitudes and communication and emotional management, but no marriage can rise to the higher plateaus without major investments of time. One of the single most common complaints I hear about distant husbands is their unwillingness to spend the time needed to simply keep in touch. Other priorities inevitably take center stage.

To women (and often to men as well), the amount of time a spouse spends on the marriage is a pretty clear barometer of that person's commitment to it. In John's case, his Beverly ran out of emotional energy begging him for his time. "I'm not a priority," she told him. "Even your fantasies outweigh my importance. I'm done trying."

And Gary? It never occurred to him to spend time with his Ruth. "There's a lot of stuff in life that you know without having to be reminded about all the time," he pouted. "I get a twenty-thousand-dollar loan, the bank doesn't have to call me up and remind me every day. I know it's there. Same with love. Ruthie doesn't have to remind me every day that she loves me. People don't need constant reminders for things they know are true."

"Spoken like a true male," I replied. "Most men don't. Many women do. It's amazing to me how men can have a much lower need for connecting time. Probably it's so much easier for us to be project-oriented. But if your marriage is to survive and flourish, you've got to invest time."

On another occasion, Howard and Lynette Sandstrom approached the same topic.

As Howard put it, "So what am I supposed to do, go home every evening and talk about deep feelings? I'm sorry. I'm not up to it. It would be like talking about, uh, opera. I know zilch about opera, and that's as much as I want to know about it. I wouldn't know what to say." He shook his head. "I don't know what Lynette wants, but whatever it is, I doubt I can deliver."

"Good!" I responded. "Why d—"

"Good?!" Lynette exploded. "Why is that statement good?"

"Because at least he's admitting the problem. Howard, why don't you take Lynette out to dinner, just the two of you, and ask her what she wants? Get details. Find out what you have to know in order to deliver. Make that your next home-improvement project, for it will certainly improve your home." Then I added, "And as she tells you what she wants, make no rebuttal. Your task is to listen and absorb, not debate."

In Gary and Ruth's case, neither Gary nor Ruth knew exactly what to do. Gary was indifferent to emotional connection, and Ruth worked so hard and so long that she had lost contact with herself. They agreed that their marriage could use a lot more closeness, but neither was certain how to attain it.

I suggested they reestablish emotional contact by scheduling three occasions in the next week for sharing.

Ruth wrinkled her nose. "'Sharing.' That word sounds trite. I hate using 'sharing.'"

"It's the best definition of what you want to do, though," I replied. "Not just tell each other something, but lay things out on the table for you to explore together."

Gary, so in love with his TV remote, looked like a dump truck was headed for him at a sixty miles an hour. "Turn off TV?"

"Sorry. Turn off TV. Put the children to bed or bar them from the room. Get a sitter for an hour."

"So what do we share?" Ruth was beginning to look hopeful.

"How about a phone call one of you received? Unpleasant news from a relative. Pleasant news. In all this, you explore not what those relatives can or can't do to better their situation, but how they feel. How you feel. Pleased, hurt, confused, happy. Ask follow-up questions. Talk about something that provoked strong feelings in you recently—but *not* the latest irritation or accusation."

"Don't get at each other's throat like usual."

"Good way to put it. You're talking about feelings, not behavior. Confessing personal shortcomings isn't a bad topic either."

Ruth grinned impishly. "And what makes you think I have any?"

How about you readers? When did you last open windows to each other?

Think about the many projects you've tackled during your adult years: learning computers, improving your golf game, serving on committees, organizing home chores. Did you accomplish any of these without a serious time commitment? Of course not! Now compare the importance of your primary relationships to these other activities. Do your relationships require anything less than your best time?

Will you run out of things to explore together? No. Whatever stage you are in, something new is evolving. The same goes for your spouse. John provides a good for-instance. In his fifty-some years, he had never before faced imminent retirement. Grandchildren? They loomed in his immediate future. These are changes generating extremely emotional responses. John would profit as greatly from time spent sharing as would his Beverly.

One of his most valuable resources, and yours, is the spouse. If time is in such short supply that you must schedule appointments with each other, so be it. But look for chances for spontaneity as well. In all this, acceptance is rather assumed, but it must be acknowledged by itself.

## Acceptance Is Primary

Once you agree that time will be an ongoing priority, you will need to determine the atmosphere that will prevail as you spend time with each other. Healthy relationships are distinguished by the willingness to offer acceptance even in the midst of differences and imperfections.

Distant husbands and emotionally eager wives alike so frequently complain that they feel acceptance is offered in low doses or with strings attached. I hear statements such as:

- "If I say or feel the wrong thing, my spouse turns off and won't have anything to do with me."
- "When I voice an opinion or preference, I can tell that my spouse is already constructing a rebuttal."
- "Lately I've had to really watch what I say and be cautious and calculated about everything."
- "My mate has too many conditions for me to meet and maintain."

Does that sound familiar to you? Ultimately, anger, defensiveness, and worry are strong indicators that acceptance is lacking. In fact, tension can be read as a protest: "Won't you *please* accept who I am!"

Ask yourself, "Am I willing to set aside my need for correctness and order long enough to accept my mate, even though I see failings or imperfections?" I am not suggesting that you maintain no standards or boundaries. For example, Jean Moreland need not in the least accept Mark's addiction, which she acknowledged as deeply sinful. But she can still accept Mark the person. I am, in other words, asking that you begin with the willingness to concede that not all will be as you mandate, and it's probably beyond your control to change.

We can say with certainty that your spouse is a mixed bag of pluses and minuses. We can also say the same about you. And while it is reasonable to discuss with your partner how each of you might improve, the truth remains that flaws as seen by the other mate are inevitable. Guaranteed. Can you live with this?

Gary told Ruth, "You know, for years I've tried to figure out what you want from me, and every time I think I about have it, it changes. No matter how I try, it's not good enough."

Ruth came back with, "So what am I supposed to do about that, quit believing there should be certain standards? Everybody has standards. Right and wrong."

"Yeah, but with you, it doesn't matter whether it's the right way or the wrong way. It's gotta be Ruthie's way. And heaven help me, or anyone else, if I don't know what Ruthie's way is and don't do it that way. I get rained on more than the Amazon."

Do you similarly suffer from the affliction of being so correct that you are incapable of accepting freely? Forgiveness is involved here, and tolerance, but it goes beyond that. Acceptance is a mind-set, a base that stems from the fact that this person is dear to you and part of you.

To establish acceptance and then to communicate it, you will need to determine for yourself that traits such as kindness, patience, and tolerance are more important than perfection or propriety. Relationship-building takes priority over conformity and obligation.

To help Gary and Ruth, and also John and Beverly, I asked,

"What about in your dating days? Did you have a rigid list of behaviors that you thought your prospective mate ought to follow? Or did you accept that person for who he was? He or she."

They all replied, "Back then it was okay."

It should still be okay. The ability to accept another person hinges directly to the understanding of one's own need for acceptance. Here is the Golden Rule in new clothes: Accept others as you would want to be accepted, in spite of flaws, weaknesses, and differences.

Let's be practical with this concept. Think for a moment about the most common incidences where a lack of acceptance was especially obvious. The most reliable clues to this nonacceptance are troublesome emotions: irritability, impatience, anxiety, and the like. The incidences triggering nonacceptance can be very common. You don't like the way your mate manages extended family matters; this was true with Ruth and Gary, you'll remember. You would prefer that your spouse express emotions differently, or perhaps not at all. You can't understand why certain "harmless" events evoke tension.

Now picture yourself in the midst of these circumstances revisited. What would you do differently if you employed a mind of acceptance? How would your words sound? What look would you have on your face? You will find that the commitment to be accepting will require awareness about the many small incidences that could easily result in irritation or offensiveness. Armed with a powerful conviction to be a positive presence in your mate's life, however, you can project a genuinely supportive demeanor.

## Respect Is Given, Not Earned

Following closely on the heels of the decision to accept is the determination to show respect.

I so often hear people say, "I'll accept others for what they are, but that doesn't mean I have to respect them. That's something that has to be earned."

Notice the implication of such a statement. You're saying that your ability to live with a healthy trait is determined by factors outside yourself. The responsibility for your positive quality rests on someone else's shoulders. That quality is reduced to a matter of reaction rather than initiative.

Would you be willing to be respectful even when another person is not openly deserving of it? Or consider the alternative. When you are disrespectful, you can clear your conscience by claiming it is not your fault, but the result of the other person's impropriety. Are you going through life blaming others for your lack of solid character traits?

Healthy relationships improve when individuals determine on their own how they will pursue positive qualities. Admittedly, the success of the relationship is greatly increased when both parties determine this simultaneously. But I am assuming that no relationship is ever so perfectly synchronized that full harmony of goals happens when everyone wants it to. Rather than allowing inconsistencies to drive your style of relating, then, you can choose your own direction independently.

Exactly what does it mean to give respect? Does it imply that you must deny painful feelings in order to maintain a pleasant demeanor? No. Respect is the acknowledgment of human value separate from performance. For instance, when a child misbehaves, you may need to reprimand him and apply consequences, yet it can be done without robbing the child of his dignity. Likewise, when your partner has disappointed or failed you, emotions and boundary considerations result; but you can still choose to refrain from indignities and condescension.

As Jean observed, "Mark's porn addiction isn't common knowledge, but his high and mighty treatment of me is. My family and friends have said more than once that they wonder how I lived with him as long as I did. When you hear things like that all the time, it makes it easier to abandon respect. What I'm saying is, you start to develop the attitude that he's a jerk who doesn't deserve extra effort, and comments from people you care about add fuel."

"Setting aside your focus on his wrongs," I suggested, "let's look at what lack of respect for Mark does to you. I'm going to assume that it draws you deeper into disillusionment and anger."

She nodded, grimacing. "You assume correctly."

"And who is the loser?"

"I am," she admitted. "He doesn't even notice."

Sometimes the wisest choice is to override the angry or hurt feeling of the moment, choosing instead to act in a civil manner. I am not suggesting the suppression or denial of feelings. I am suggesting that they need not govern the way you act. Your feelings, remember, can be driven by selfish motives. Be careful.

Disrespect generates disrespect—the Golden Rule in still another guise.

What does it mean to maintain, in the midst of reality, respect that has not been earned? Let me offer some common examples:

■ Your spouse, rude and insulting, calls you names. It's not the first time. You determine that you will not let your mate pull you down to that level of response.

■ You are hurt or disappointed, so you say so. Respect requires that you refrain from coercion and shrill accusation.

■ Despite your best efforts, your spouse lives counter to your preferences. Respect recognizes that person's freedom to be wrong. Note that this does not mean there are never consequences, but it does recognize that dictatorial "bossiness" won't work.

Being respectful in the midst of unpleasant circumstances isn't easy. To sustain your ability to live with this quality, remember: You can choose to be as ugly as you like in the way you treat others. Don't let anyone tell you disrespect is not an option, because it is. But before you run with that thought, also remember who the loser will be when you consistently choose disrespect. You. Let your attitudes be guided by your finest beliefs, not another's worst behavior.

## Blame Is Replaced with Insight

A consistent pattern emerges in almost all initial sessions I conduct with people experiencing relationship breakdowns. I will hear elaborate explanations detailing what others have done to bring about tension. Most of these explanations have strong elements of truth, so I cannot fault the persons telling me about their disappointments in others. In most cases, I'd feel hurt or angry or discouraged if I, too, had to live with the pain described.

The cases that stagnate, though, are the ones in which the individuals insist that they cannot find healthiness until the wrongdoers correct their ways. When I try to shift the focus onto their own choices, these people will resist by putting it right back upon the wrongdoers in their life.

Is it wrong to examine the motives of people who have hurt you? Or to understand how your historical circumstances affect your current life? Not at all. Your enlightenment about the people around you can result in objectivity, the ability to understand facts without also becoming emotionally drawn into them.

One of the first things we do in counseling, usually, is to explore the past to find out what clients learned about dealing with the self. John and Howard learned by example from their parents to put work projects first and relegate emotional needs to the bottom of the list. In order to overcome the learned trait of getting priorities backward, they needed reminders of where they learned it.

Now consider this. By understanding these insights, based upon analysis of the past, does that excuse the people in counseling from taking responsibility for their poor methods of relating? There's a reason they don't do it right; therefore, they can conclude, "No wonder I'm no good at maintaining relationships. Look what others have done to me!" How handy blame can be!

I see counselees stuck in this place frequently. And as you look at it with any degree of detachment at all, you see that getting stuck should never have happened. Understanding the past is a key for opening the gate to improvement; it's never a cop-out.

As you gain understanding regarding the problems surrounding you, be descriptive in your assessment but not judgmental. Ultimately, blame involves judgment, which is not a quality likely to help relationships grow.

What is the purpose behind judgments in a marriage? What do they accomplish? Usually, the person who blames has felt that he or she has been relegated to a position of inferiority. Unwilling to remain on the low end of relationships, they yearn to be superior as compensation. That is where blame enters the picture. They are compensating for low feelings by thinking "superior" thoughts. For a brief time, satisfaction can come as the other person squirms in discomfort.

But notice what happens next. When you treat your spouse in an inferior way, he or she will try to get the upper hand through whatever means will work—counterattack, punishment, pouting, withdrawal. A seesaw effect is set off with ever-escalating consequences. The competition is on to determine who will be above the other.

By refraining from blame, you are choosing to operate on level ground. You can acknowledge faults, needs, misgivings, but without turning discussions into battles of one-upmanship.

What blaming tendencies do you have that you would be willing to dismiss? When your mate discusses one of your faults, can you hear without retaliating? Can you also describe the factors that play into your imperfections without projecting a harsh image or demeanor?

"You mean it's never anyone else's fault?" John didn't seem to be buying all this about blame.

"I'm not saying you are wrong in conclusions you draw. I'm saying that if you use your awareness of others' faults as a club, you've failed to capitalize on the insights you've gained. It pays to be as constructive as possible in dealing with problems. Blame is not constructive."

## Openness Is Highly Valued

In the beginning chapter, we identified the lack of account-ability on the part of the distant, evasive husband's contribution to marital stress. Sometimes this can become so prominent that a game of "cops and robbers" can exist in the marriage.

To counter this trend, openness is required. When a man and woman commit to marriage, they are committing to unity. While still two very different personalities, they are one in the sense that they now have the same goals of encouraging each other, meeting personal needs, and tackling life together. When one or both keep secrets or hold the other at bay, that oneness is lost.

The case of Jean and Mark illustrates this. Mark maintained heavy, heavy secrets. See how they shattered the unity? Secrets always, always do that; theirs is simply an extreme case of a general rule.

Howard and Lynette present another aspect. Howard pretty much entered his marriage with his guard up. He determined from childhood on that mistakes and feelings were not the world's business. The gaps in his marriage widened as resentment replaced tenderness.

And Gary and Ruth. I suggested to them, "Let's try a nothing-to-lose position. Keeping each other at bay will only result in more of the same distancing. Can you two disclose to each other that you are determined to lay down your defenses?"

Gary looked hesitant. "I'm not the kind who can just naturally talk about what I feel. Sure, I admit there are times I should talk about personal stuff with Ruthie, but . . ." He shrugged. "But."

Ruth twisted in her chair to face him. "Oh, come on! When did you ever want to talk about anything personal?"

"Like when my father died, for instance."

She stared. "You blew that off like it was no big deal to you! You were back on a construction site the day after the funeral. And the kids! They just lost their grandfather, and you didn't even try to comfort them. How were we supposed to know that you wanted to talk, when you were hiding behind that ten-foot cement-block wall?"

"It seems," I inserted, "that this illustration is an example of how your closed, truncated style of communication breeds tension and wrong assumptions. Do you see how openness at the time would have prevented this acrimony?"

"Acrimony." Gary wrinkled his nose. "Isn't that what divorced men have to pay?"

Ruth snickered, "Oh get off it. You know what acrimony means. See? We're trying to talk some deep stuff here, and you're blowing it off again, with humor."

"Now wait." I raised a hand. "You both feel comfortable when you're making puns and jokes. And comfort is a very necessary element in openness. You can't be open if you feel extremely uncomfortable. If Gary—or you, Ruth—uses humor to lighten a situation and bring it closer to his comfort zone, there's not a thing wrong with that. Deep, serious meanings clothed in a lighter mood—sometimes that can help."

"Sugarcoating the pill."

"If that's what it takes."

Gary asked, "What if she laughs at me?"

"I thought that was the purpose of humor."

"No, I mean, what if she laughs at my feelings, or . . . you know."

"It's a risk. You two might want to make clear promises about that beforehand."

Gary pressed on. "And what if I lose it; I mean, get on some emotional tractor I can't get off of?"

Ruth answered that. "So big deal. You break down and cry. We're talking private here, not the whole world watching on television. There are some things in life that crying helps, you know. Like mourning your father. He was a great old man, Gary."

And Gary broke down and cried.

*To the Husband.* How about you? As the husband, are you willing to take the leadership in creating a more open and comfortable home atmosphere? Are you willing to lay aside your protective barriers and get serious about loving your wife?

*To the Wife.* And you. Are you committed to making the home a safer place for your mate? Will you refrain from judgment? Can you listen and express your needs without acrimony?

Husband and wife together can listen all day long to the how-tos of a safer and more comfortable marriage. Success will come when you fix upon the goal of making a better marriage and each adopts a "count me in" mind-set.

But what if one mate or the other refuses to cooperate? Let's look at that next.

## chapter 10

# *W*hat If
# He
# Won't Change?

*I*begin this chapter with an admission of frustration. I can talk with people at great length about the ways to find personal and relational happiness, but I am limited in my ability to make it happen in the lives of the people hearing me. Often, wives will bring their husbands into counseling with the thought, "Maybe this guy can be the one to get through to my husband. Maybe he can make him see the light, and we'll have a better life." They are hoping that my power will be just the thing to create the harmony they so desperately desire.

Honestly, I wish I were such a miracle worker. When talking with men about being more responsive to their wives' needs, I'll give it everything I've got. We will go about the business of identifying nonproductive patterns of behavior and communications. We will explore the reasons why their emotions and behaviors are slanted as they are. We will discuss the need for a delicate understanding of the wife's very different feelings. We will spell out alternatives.

When it is all said and done, though, the rest of the change process is determined by a solitary factor: How powerfully does the husband want to change?

Lynette sat in front of me looking as if she were attending a funeral. And maybe in some respects that is exactly what she might have to do, attend the funeral of her own marriage.

She sighed heavily. "How long have we been doing this? Six months?" She raised her hands in a gesture of helplessness. "Nothing's really changed. When Howard was coming I thought there might be hope. Then he quit."

"No easing of tensions at all?"

She shook her head. "He tried for a couple of weeks; at least, I guess he tried. Now it's all back to the way it was, the way it's been for most of our marriage. He avoids talking about anything he thinks hints of depth or psychological meaning. If anything, he seems to be avoiding me more. Know what he says now whenever I try to tell him something? 'Good! Good. That's nice. I imagine you're happy about it.' He doesn't mean it. Doesn't mean a word of it. He doesn't even think about what he said. He figures saying that will get me off his back.

"I hate having to accept defeat! But what am I going to do?" Tears glistened. "He's never going to change. Never."

## ON YOUR OWN

"Defeat? That's unfair." I shook my head. "You can claim defeat only if you made no effort, or if you hadn't grown and changed yourself. Okay, the results aren't what you set out to achieve, but as far as your efforts and intentions go, you're a winner still."

A lot of wives can relate to Lynette's predicament. Perhaps you are one of them. I genuinely hope that your attempts to understand your needs and how they developed, as well as your husband's behaviors and how they developed, will result in improved camaraderie. But if you feel as frustrated as Lynette, and as I do when my efforts with clients end in incomplete outcomes, you still have options. Don't give up on yourself!

In your search for marital improvement, have you given it your best shot so far? Here's a little quiz to help answer that question. Check those statements that pertain to you.

_____ 1. My attempts to bring about an improved marriage have been accompanied by prayer.

_____ 2. While I can identify the areas my spouse should improve, I have also become aware of my own contributions that damage our relating.

_____ 3. For the most part, I try to communicate my needs and feelings without pressing too hard or becoming accusing or coercive.

_____ 4. I realize my well-being cannot revolve around only one person. I have developed a good support system.

_____ 5. I have developed a better sense of timing when it comes to opening a discussion of a sensitive subject.

_____ 6. Even when I'm strongly disappointed, I tend to be an encourager. I am known for my willing spirit.

_____ 7. I realize that self-pity doesn't help a bit. Although I cannot suppress my own needs and desires, I also understand that brooding and complaining won't do any good.

_____ 8. When I'm with friends and relatives, I try to avoid speaking poorly about my spouse.

_____ 9. I'm what is called an eager learner. I enjoy the stimulation of provocative reading and discussion.

_____ 10. I try to remain approachable, and I am open to any feedback my spouse might offer regarding our relationship.

_____ 11. I genuinely desire for my mate to express himself freely, even if it feels uncomfortable to him or to me.

_____ 12. I have been making strong efforts to understand why my spouse thinks and feels as he does.

Chances are, you cannot check every item. If you did, you'd be nearly perfect, which is very difficult when you are locked in a disappointing relationship that has a way of exposing your own weaknesses. Nonetheless, the more items you are able to check, the better you can hold your head high in the realization that you're coping as well as you know how. Carefully rethink the items you did not check. Can you work some improvement there as well?

When I talk to people like Lynette who have concluded that, short of a miracle, their efforts are going to avail little or nothing, I suggest several key concepts that can bring personal improvement. Let's take a look at several of them.

## Think About Your Emotional Growth in Singular Terms

In counseling, when I see that a wife is pressing too hard to find marital harmony, I say something that at first glance seems odd to her. "Don't make increased marital harmony your primary goal." But then, as she looks at me as if I just defected to the enemy, I add, "Instead, make personal healthiness your primary goal. Then, if marital improvement happens, it will be a welcome by-product of your efforts."

Understand I am not suggesting to these women that they should assume a selfish, me-first mentality. That would be going too far to the other extreme. Instead, I am operating on the belief that the husband will not change unless he wants to. If improvement comes, it will be the result of his desire, not the wife's coercion.

Let's put a perspective on this. Most people like to say that marriage is a 50-50 proposition where each person contributes equally to its success. But when failures occur, which 50 percent are you most likely to focus upon? Or let's suppose you say, "Okay. It's an 80-20 proposition. I'll shoulder 80 percent of the burden for making the relationship work." In moments of difficulty, you'll still be tempted to say, "I'm carrying 80 percent. What are you doing with your 20?"

Simply put, when you say, "We need to change," it often filters over to mean, "You've got to do your part just like I'm doing." Then comes blame, defense, criticism, and so on.

This is how I put it to Lynette. "As much as I'd like to see you and Howard have a fully satisfying and happy life together, I don't want to see you become an ineffectual, even say miserable person because of his marital style. As you look back through the years, you'll discover that your continuing focus on 'us' has provided enough heartache that you've lost a great deal of happiness. You can't afford that."

"I don't see any way out."

Hear the loneliness buried in that admission of resignation. "Sometimes the truth can make you feel isolated. You want so badly to be connected to Howard at the deepest level that you press for it even in the face of mounting evidence that it's never going to happen."

Lynette looked near tears. "All I ever really wanted was to be a successful wife and mother. I mean a really good one. Do you realize how much it hurts to admit I failed?"

"What's this 'failed' business? Howard refuses to connect intimately. That does not in any way detract from the fact that you've been there for him even in the absence of emotional encouragement. And besides: You have to remember that he'd be the same kind of husband no matter whom he married. He's his person; you're yours. You can't change that. You can recognize your own success when you focus on your own contribution rather than the presence or absence of adjustments you think he ought to make."

Certainly, it's unrealistic to have zero expectations, but keeping expectations minimal decreases the wife's frustration and bitterness. I encourage any woman to make the contribution she wants to a successful married life regardless of his efforts or lack of them.

The husband is half the team, true. But the wife ought not to get so sidetracked in trying to make him look good that she forgets her own goals. Given Howard's lack of interest in relational growth, Lynette should stay focused on being personally healthy, then consider it an unexpected bonus if his desire for intimacy eventually improves.

## Keep Balance When Publicly Disclosing Your Pain

If you are in a marriage that is not producing the satisfaction, let alone bliss, that you had once anticipated, will you feel hurt? Disillusioned? Angry? Of course you will! You are human, and you cannot force yourself to dismiss these emotions.

When women experience the pain of a less-than-wonderful relationship, they are often caught in a dilemma. How honest should they be with themselves and others regarding what they are experiencing emotionally? Most of these wives float between one of two extremes. Either they assume they should say little or nothing about their problems as they attempt to keep up a good front, or they talk too much to anyone who will listen. Either extreme needs to be avoided.

Lynette grimaced. "I had this acquaintance once—I call her acquaintance; she'd probably call me a friend—whose honesty really turned me off. If someone said something complimentary about her husband, she'd instantly show them how they were wrong and he wasn't really as nifty as they thought. She loved to tell us about her latest fights. In the end, it seemed that she loved being at odds with him. Like it was a sick relationship of some sort." She looked at me, seeming a bit ashamed. "But you know, I envied her in a way. She was saying things I couldn't."

Most of the time, Lynette wore a polite mask in public. Should anyone ask, even obliquely, she'd simply smile and say how fine everything was. As she explained, "When he and I are out together someplace, I wouldn't want the people we were with to think we were misfits. There's enough gossip without adding to it."

So which is best? Cover up? Or be frankly honest?

Neither and both. Let's strike a realistic balance here. One goal is genuineness, the lack of pretense, the presence of honesty. But this should be wisely tempered by the wisdom that you cannot be fully disclosing to every person.

There are different levels of friendship, and those persons who occupy the more superficial or casual levels need not know all your highs and lows. But there is also a deep, satisfying level of friendship that most women enjoy with perhaps four or five others at most. These friendships do not occur predictably, but you know them when they happen. Lynette's bosom-friendship with Kris is an example. These are the friends you can trust with deep thoughts and even secrets. They don't blab, they don't judge, they don't laugh.

And then there is the great middle ground. These are the friends and acquaintances whom you know fairly well. With them, you don't want to lie, saying how wonderful life is if it is not, but neither need you go into elaborate and ugly detail.

As Lynette said, "I usually try to make things sound fine because I don't want anyone to think we're the kind of people who can't work out problems. I guess I want everyone to think we have our act together all the time."

That's natural. And it certainly takes some of the pressure off when you can admit openly that the relationship is not always perfect. Basically, you will do a balancing act between generating gossip and suffering the pressure of trying to project the image of perfection.

Just knowing that you have permission to be imperfect will make life more relaxed. You can't live happily ever after trying to look like something you're not.

## You Needn't Always Run Interference for Your Husband

That includes making your man out to be something he is not or cushioning him or others from himself.

Ruth Sweeney provided an excellent example. Her Gary and his mom rarely saw eye to eye. Ruth, on the other hand, was quite comfortable with her mother-in-law. Ruth reported this exchange:

The mother-in-law, Emma, called Ruth on Monday morning. "Tell Gary that Frank is very upset because Gary didn't invite him over last weekend with the guys from the construction crew.

Frank has so many problems just now, and his brother isn't helping any."

Ruth reported the conversation to Gary at lunchtime.

Gary waved a hand on his way out the door, headed back to work. "Frank's a jerk. If he wants some friends, he can go make them. He's not going to keep borrowing mine."

Ruth reported Gary's response to Emma that afternoon as, "Gary said he was sorry. He didn't think to ask his brother because Frank doesn't work for that crew. Next time I'll remind him."

Smooth over. Cover up. Excuse away. How very often a wife does that! Ruth not only acted as go-between, she recast Gary's attitude into something she hoped would be more palatable to his mother.

Distant or evasive husbands particularly can invite protective behavior. They seem to invite opportunities. For instance:

- Your husband is not attuned to your daughter's feelings, so you constantly try to reinterpret his actions, hoping the daughter will be less hurt by the apparent snubs or callousness.
- The extended family doesn't know how to take your husband's moods, so they bring their complaints to you, and you excuse the behavior away with various explanations.
- You dislike his treatment of certain friends and feel free to mend bridges by privately providing the friends with explanations for his behavior.

What's behind this need to patch up damage that your mate's behavior, words, and attitude may have inadvertently caused? There are a few factors.

Sometimes, the wife has a legitimate concern that his flawed character is a poor representation of hers. An example might be a social event by the company she works for. Her boss and coworkers may measure her in part by the behavior of her spouse. After all, she chose him as a marriage partner. If he acts in contrary ways, she runs the risk of others assuming she shares those flaws. She might be wrongly judged.

But more commonly, the temptation to run interference is tied to the wife's desire to be in control. She wishes she could control her man's behavior. But that is impossible, so she embarks on the next best thing—tidying up how his behavior looks (and indirectly, how hers does).

Ruth sniffed. "Gary's behavior doesn't need tidying, it needs steam-cleaning. He really does snub his brother. And it really does hurt his mom. What am I supposed to do?"

You probably already know what my answer was. "Nothing."

"But isn't that really cold and cruel on my part?"

"What did Frank, Emma, and Gary do before you married him?"

"Crabbed at each other. Fought a lot."

"If that relationship is going to change, who has to change it?"

Ruth said most reluctantly, "They do."

"Are you familiar with the term *enabling*?"

"Yeah, where you cover for a person with an addiction or bad habit so that he can keep going in the addiction. Or habit. He or she. Whatever."

"So if you step back and cease enabling, what will happen with Gary and his relatives?"

Ruth chuckled. "Crab at each other and fight a lot. So what do I do instead?"

Some suggestions:

- Get out of the middle. When Ruth's mother-in-law called with her complaint, Ruth would not have been out of line to say, simply, "Gary and you are adults. You're going to have to discuss this between you."
- Toss the ball back into the other court. Emma makes her complaint. Ruth responds with, "What will you do about it, Emma?"
- Make it clear that you will take care of your own emotions and

relationships and others must tend to theirs. Then stick to your guns.

Ruth did not seem thoroughly convinced. "I thought I was supposed to be supportive."

"That's not nonsupport. That's giving the others in your world the responsibility and privilege to think and act for themselves. Denying them that is not in their best interests. Don't take a responsibility that should not be yours to shoulder."

## Guard Against Your Vulnerability to Other Men

When the Sandstroms' church needed someone to spearhead their weekend fair, whom would they call but Lynette, who did such a splendid job with the PTA auction? She cleared it with Howard, who generally took a dim view of his phone ringing on weekends. He acquiesced. She had a job.

She began the planning process the day after she accepted.

"It's over six months away!" Howard protested, incredulous.

"I know that's not much time, but I think I can do it."

As Howard watched her scurry out the door, he perceived that this was going to be another of her projects that he described as "marathon masochism."

Adept at assembling committees, Lynette chose five persons she knew had interests in the five major fair activities. For instance, one of those five, a veterinarian named Walker Tayes, took on the pet parade, the small children's petting zoo, and the dog, cat, and horse shows.

"That's a lot," Lynette said dubiously. "Are you sure you want to take that big a bite?"

Walker grinned. "I've done some of this before. Besides, I know every animal in the county." He raised one finger. "Oh, and Lynette. Never use the word *bite* around a veterinarian."

Walker was as good at organizing as Lynette was. He got the pet parade marching right along—his pun. It took him a week to arrange the petting zoo, including a deal with a local feed store to provide little bags of cracked corn. He ask some of his clients, teenaged girls who owned horses, to set up the shows. "Eager" is understating their response. What impressed Lynette most was Walker's easy, open humor. When everything appeared to be crashing down wrong, he would get it going right again with a relentlessly cheerful spirit.

As the date neared, Lynette scheduled weekly committee meetings to keep everything on track, adjusting loads and filling gaps. One such evening after the meeting, when all but Walker had left, the two of them sat around in the church kitchen until midnight, sipping coffee and talking. Just talking. She vented her frustrations with Howard. He revealed his frustrations with his wife, a cool and humorless woman.

So here they were, a sensitive, funny, professional man who was everything Howard was not, and a warm, bright woman who was everything Mrs. Tayes was not. Recipe for disaster? Absolutely! Many times in my practice, I see people much less suited to each other become involved in extramarital affairs.

Most women enter marriage expecting to be consistently affirmed, and that is as it should be. Affirmation is immensely important to every human being. When that necessary affirmation does not come from the husband, the woman is vulnerable to receiving it from outside the union. If the affirming person is male instead of female, she becomes spectacularly vulnerable.

Temptation can grip even more tightly if the woman grew up with many of the insecurities and emotional deficiencies discussed in earlier chapters. An evasive, distant husband who possesses his own insecurities and emotional deficiencies can't help the woman grow much.

The vast majority of women who find themselves in an extramarital affair are more shocked and surprised by the turn of events than are any of their friends.

- "How could this happen to me?"
- "Believe me, neither of us intended for this to happen!"
- "I'm a sensible Christian woman. I assumed I was immune."

No one is immune. No one. Let me shout that to the skies: *No one is immune!* The moment you assume immunity, you're letting your guard down. The moment you assume you're too sensible to make so foolish a mistake, you're letting your guard down.

I suggest four means of minimizing temptation. One is to never let your guard down. Keep an eye out for red flags. The second is to discuss intimate matters only with a trusted *female* friend or professional counselor. Sharing deep personal matters brings about bonding that can lead to deeper connections than are safe. The third is to avoid situations that could escalate. The fourth is to seek accountability.

There were red flags aplenty in the growing relationship between Lynette and Walker. Lynette certainly considered herself immune. One red flag. Lynette found in Walker a confidant for her deepest thoughts and feelings. Another red flag. They had ample opportunity to talk alone, such as following meetings. Lynette also met separately with her committee chairs, Walker among them. Still another red flag.

Yes, you protest, but she had no choice. She can't quit relating to anyone who is male just because she's vulnerable. It was appropriate to meet separately with her animal chair, so to speak, when such meetings were needed.

And that's right. Such contact cannot be avoided. I do say it must be monitored with caution. Staying late and chatting was dangerous. Bringing the conversation to an intimate, emotional level was dangerous. Both of those situations should have been avoided.

Accountability? Kris was the natural person for Lynette to use. In fact, Lynette had on two occasions served Kris in that way. Kris, too, was tempted. Wisely, she asked Lynette to stay nosy. In return she had to promise always to be honest. If Lynette asked her what was happening and how it was going, she had to be truthful. It kept her out of immorality on both occasions.

I've learned another thing from my years of counseling with thousands of couples: No matter how empty the woman feels, an affair does not fill the emotional holes. Period. Never. For a brief time in the beginning, it seems that it does. Here is the answer to this woman's pain, loneliness, and dearth of communication. But deception and manipulation take their toll. They eat her alive. Suicidal ideation is a surprisingly frequent fruit of an extramarital affair, particularly if the affair becomes common knowledge among her friends.

Did Lynette fall? No. It was Kris who spotted trouble on the immediate horizon and woke her up with a stern lecture delivered with loving concern. But she came so close to making the error of a lifetime.

## Know When to Forgive

We've talked a lot about anger in this book. But I may not have emphasized how wives of distant husbands often harbor immense reservoirs of anger. These women married with high hopes for a lifetime of friendship and encouragement. It hasn't happened, at least not adequately. Those dreams seem out of reach now. Anger results.

The best vent of anger is simply an ongoing communication of feelings, needs, and perceptions. When the man and wife succeed in keeping each other abreast of these things, they are probably going to maintain manageable anger levels.

Wives of distant, evasive, uninvolved husbands don't have that advantage. They try every trick they can think of to coerce their men into doing something while their men try every trick they can think of to avoid it. Unwilling to accept the inevitable, these women usually make one of two mistakes. They continue to pressure the husband, with increasingly negative results, or they allow resentment to build within themselves. Distrust and depression follow.

If your husband, like Lynette's, won't change, you can most likely relate to the emotional turmoil Lynette and others must deal with. And it's very tiresome!

The time comes, sooner or later, when Ruth, Lynette, and

perhaps you must be willing to admit the truth regarding their mates' nonavailability and forgive. They and you need to recognize that bitterness and tension can be a chosen path but forgiveness is also a chosen path.

"I'm sorry." Lynette sounded adamant. "Howard isn't just being passively insensitive. Now he's actively evading my needs. I cannot condone or accept his behavior. It's totally unacceptable to me. And that's what forgiveness is—condoning. No." She wagged her head and repeated, "No. I'm sorry."

I asked, "What has the pressure you've tried so far netted you? Are you closer now to the goal of connecting with Howard on a more intimate level than you were a year ago?"

"Well, uh . . ."

"Any sign of progress?"

Lynette admitted, "The opposite, if anything."

"I rest my case."

"But I will *not* condone! I will *not* admit defeat!"

Let's pause here and pick forgiveness apart. Let's look at what it is and what it is not.

Forgiveness is not:

- Giving in. It is recognition of the stalemate.
- An admission of defeat. By no means are you planning to just throw in the towel.
- Condoning or even accepting. Those are other issues, other matters.
- Abandoning your convictions. You still know what you want.
- Evidence of an "Aw, who cares?" attitude. You care deeply!

Forgiveness is:

- Recognition of your inability to control his nature and opinions.
- Part of a commitment to your own peace of mind, not his.
- Your choice to set aside anger, not because anger is wrong but because it's not doing any good.

- A willingness to let God take over, perhaps to exact discipline, where your efforts have fallen short.

Let's get practical. Think about incidents in your marriage that repeatedly fuel your anger, especially problems that crop up over and over again despite your many efforts to remedy them. Here are some random examples I commonly come across:

- His rudeness to extended family, especially yours.
- His desire to be a fun daddy, but not a disciplinarian, leaving the unpleasant aspects of parenting to you.
- His cavalier disinterest in your needs and activities.
- His tightness with money.
- His unwillingness to talk with you about deep or personal matters.
- His temper.

The list could go on and on, but you get the point.

Now consider what you would be like in the midst of these circumstances if you chose forgiveness. How would you speak? What attitude would you project? What thoughts would wander unspoken in your mind? It's not an easy assignment, is it!

A client we'll call Karen, representing many, many women who air this complaint, was hurt by the way her Patrick related to her in contrast to the way he related to the rest of the world.

Said Karen, "In public, he's Mr. Charm. He can cajole a Republican into voting Democrat. He's always, always pleasant. At home, in private, he doesn't have a good word to say to me. Grumpy, critical, demanding, sour. I can't stand it!"

I understood. "It leaves you feeling that either he's manipulating everyone else or that he likes everyone but you. I'm going to assume that this means he is confused about how to manage relationships, and what is worse, he isn't really trying to change."

For Karen to forgive Patrick, she had first to specifically define for herself exactly what she was forgiving. In this case it was his emotional immaturity, his treatment of her, and even, perhaps, his false front. She had to acknowledge all this fairly, as it existed. She would forgive him and clearly express her forgiveness. When she could honestly pray, "God, he's in your hands. I release control of the whole situation to You," she would know the forgiveness was complete.

Did she have to give up speaking the truth with him? Certainly not. Neither did she have to become a doormat. But she did need to give Patrick to God, because change was totally beyond her control. Let Patrick be responsible for accepting or rejecting the goading of conscience that would be of God.

## Be Very Cautious About Considering Separation or Divorce

I am not naive. I know that divorce is a common outcome in marriages typified by extreme evasiveness. And there are times, as when severe problems of abuse, addiction, or adultery exist, when the decision to separate is regrettably a better option than is staying in a dangerous and completely fractured relationship.

From this point on, let us assume that I am not talking about those cases where the woman's life and safety are in danger. And incidentally, longitudinal studies show that when the husband philanders, the wife is at much higher risk for reproductive system problems in addition to the obvious—infection by a venereal disease. Other infections, even cancers, occur at higher rates in chaste women whose husbands play around. From now on, I am talking about the husband and wife where evasiveness and distancing are the primary problems. We are automatically excepting extreme cases such as physical abuse.

If you are at the point of contemplating separation or divorce, rather than asking, "How can I do this and maintain a good reputation?" ask instead, "Have I given my best effort to make the marriage work, or is there more I could do?"

You want an end to this pain. That's understandable. But, would divorce be the end of your pain or the beginning of a new kind of pain? Unless the circumstances are quite extreme, nearly every woman who divorces sooner or later claims, "I have traded one set of problems for a new set."

Why? Because you cannot automatically assume that a change in external circumstances will solve your emotional pain. A divorcee told me, "When I divorced, I thought I'd finally find relief for my misery. But my second marriage isn't meeting expectations any better than the first. Now I see that I was really mixed up and emotionally very needy before I ever married, and I was putting too much stock in the hope that my husband would fix everything."

Can her situation be fixed, as she put it? It probably cannot be made perfect, but it can be vastly improved. Quite probably, so can yours.

Certainly, never ever consider separation until you've thoroughly explored professional counseling. Counseling can help you explore needs and feelings that keep you stuck in harmful patterns of behavior. Counseling can reveal blind spots in your own makeup that need to be seen for what they are. If your husband joins you in this, wonderful! But keep in mind that counseling is for your benefit. Embrace it not as half a team, if the other half refuses to take part, but as a person who needs help. You can learn to manage the life you have now.

Accept the challenge to be the healthiest individual you can be. As you know that you are in a persistent pattern of growth and maturation, you will be most likely to respond best to whatever your husband does.

# *A*ppendix

## CHAPTER 1
## Polar-Opposite Spouses

Let's explore further the seven indicators of a struggling relationship.

**1.** Communication is reduced to power plays.

Power can be communicated in many different ways. What are four or five ways you and your spouse show power in marital communication? (For instance: "I can be stubbornly quiet," or "I will speak my opinions forcefully," or "We both specialize in rebutting the other's accusations or claims.")

**2.** One or both avoid personal accountability.

What are some common circumstances in which either of you dislikes revealing or discussing personal matters. (For instance: "I don't like disscussing money matters," or "I'll only give details about my day up to the level at which I'm questioned.")

**3.** Leadership roles are confused.

What is your idea of the role of leadership in marriage? Should the husband be "commander in chief"? How strongly should the wife express her convictions?

What could you do to ensure more clearly established roles regarding the way leadership decisions are handled? (For instance: "I need to let my mate know more clearly when I require help.")

**4.** Relationships are secondary to performance.

What accomplishments, chores, or duties take highest priority in your schedule?

How about your spouse's priorities?

How might the emphasis on performance be curtailed as you make an effort to be more relational?

**5.** Sexual relating is out of sync.

Describe your idea of satisfying sexual relations. (For instance, do you think primarily in terms of frequency? Emotional intensity? Pure physical pleasure?)

6. Personal insights are unequal.

Growing couples not only have goals regarding their relationship, they have taken the time to develop a philosophy of relating. What do you want your spouse to know about your relating philosophy that seems misunderstood? (For instance: "We need more emphasis on the spiritual dimension in our life," or "I believe encouragement needs to be foremost in our relations.")

7. Victim feelings are common.

When have you felt victimized by your spouse?

Is there anything ongoing in your marriage that makes you feel that mistreatment may continue? (For instance: "We're too volatile in our tempers," or "No one knows how hurt I've felt about certain events [specify some of them].")

## CHAPTER 2
## Starting the Awareness Process

1. It's easier to focus on the other person's need to change than to examine your own imperfections. How do you do this? (For instance: "I'm easily critical," or "I offer advice easily but don't receive it well.")

**2.** How might your marriage be different if you put a higher priority on your own need for growth? (For instance: "I'd be more humble," or "We'd have fewer prosecutor-defender exchanges.")

**3.** How can you maintain your resolve if your mate does not show the same willingness for self-examination? (For instance: "I can have a same-sex accountability partner away from the marriage.")

**4.** Look over the twenty items listed in the evasiveness inventory. Which four or five items stand out most in your home?

**5.** Now examine the twenty items of the emotionally eager inventory. Which four or five items stand out most from this list?

**6.** As you recognize your imperfect contributions to the marriage, what four or five goals could you set as you seek improvement? (For instance: "I would be less coercive in my speech," or "I need to be more revealing regarding my feelings and needs.")

7. Can you cite some common circumstances in which you and your mate interact codependently—that is, you feed negatively off each other's imperfections? (For instance: "When my mate becomes irritable, I jump in with my own irritability.")

# CHAPTER 3
## His Performance Focus

1. Performance and achievement are natural parts of life that cannot be ignored. How can you determine, though, if the performance focus is unbalanced in your marriage? (For instance: "When we stay so busy that we don't address pressing emotional needs.")

2. Looking back over the performance inventory, which three or four items stand out most in your home?

3. What experiences in your husband's childhood years may have taught him to place performance over relationships? (For instance: "He was driven to excel in sports," or "He was never encouraged to discuss emotions.")

**4.** How does the competitive spirit in your home influence your marital communications? (For instance: "Our communication is often an effort at one-upmanship," or "My spouse talks about his successes but not his failures.")

**5.** An achiever likes recognition for successful efforts. What does your spouse do when you fail to give him what he considers adequate recognition? (For instance: "He'll call his achievement to attention," or "He'll pretend he doesn't care, but I can see that he resents it.")

**6.** If you both were to pay less attention to performance and more attention to personal matters, where would you begin? (For instance: "We'd actually talk about personal feelings.")

**7.** What is your idea of tender communication? (For instance: "Paying compliments," or "Revealing hurts.")

## CHAPTER 4
## Her Feel-First Focus

1. You can't deny the reality of your emotions. They are a colorful part of your personality. How can you determine if emotions have too powerful a hold on you? (For instance: "When simple conversations turn into agitations," or "When I'm constantly second-guessing myself.")

2. Men and women do not respond to emotions the same way. How is this illustrated in your home? (For instance: "I fret easily, and my mate is so laid back that nothing bothers him.")

3. Go back over the checklist about emotions. Which three or four items apply most commonly to you?

4. When do you allow emotions to play too strong a role as you interpret your circumstances? (For instance: "If my spouse has to work late, I immediately wonder if he doesn't want to be around me.")

**5.** Emotions can cause people to react first and initiate later. When are you likely to do this to the point that it creates unnecessary turmoil? (For instance: "If the kids are moody, I become too easily caught up in their problems.")

**6.** When is your emotional nature most likely to benefit your marital harmony? (For instance: "I laugh easily," or "I can slow down long enough to hear someone else's hurt.")

**7.** What emotional need do you want your mate to be most aware of? (For instance: "I need tolerance at those times when I'm angry," or "I deeply appreciate encouraging gestures.")

## CHAPTER 5
## His Anger Imbalances

**1.** What are the common ways your husband expresses anger? (For instance: "He's not at all quiet. He can explode," or "When he's angry or frustrated, he wants everyone to leave him alone.")

**2.** Recall the purpose of anger—self-preservation. When your spouse is angry, what self-preserving needs lie behind the emotion? (For instance: "He's preserving his need for respect," or "He wants to feel heard.")

**3.** How was anger handled in your childhood home, and how does that impact you today? (For instance: "My father was chronically grouchy, so I quickly weary of my husband's similar moods.")

**4.** Looking back over the anger inventory in this chapter, which three or four items apply most specifically in your home?

**5.** What adjustments could your spouse make to help you create a less angry atmosphere? (For instance: "It would help if my opinions were not so quickly invalidated," or "I'd like more help with menial tasks.")

**6.** How can you adjust if your spouse does not grow in the fashion you'd like? (For instance: "I could have less stringent expectations," or "I need to be more forgiving.")

**7.** Anger is closely related to the desire for control. Even if your husband continues to act controlling, how can you keep this from turning into an ongoing power play? (For instance: "If he criticizes me on my parenting style, I can recognize that he has a right to his opinion. I won't try to talk him out of his perception.")

## CHAPTER 6
## Her Open Fretting

1. What circumstances most commonly cause you to fret? (For instance: "When we are under a time crunch," or "Visiting with relatives who are known to be insensitive.")

2. What impact does fretting have on the overall style of communication in your home? (For instance: "We readily deteriorate into petty bickering," or "It gives us an excuse to withdraw.")

3. Looking over the checklist about fretting, which three or four items apply commonly to you?

4. When are you *too* concerned about your responsibilities? (For instance: "I can't let church friends know I'm operating on overload," or "I worry too much about keeping family members' spirits lifted.")

5. The lack of fretting implies that you trust your ability to handle stress. How would this self-directed trust positively affect your communication? (For instance: "I'd feel less need to have my ideas validated by others.")

**6.** Too often, fretting is caused by feelings of victimization. How can you determine if your feelings of victimization are realistic or exaggerated? (For instance: "I know I'm balanced when I'm not also expecting others to make me feel good.")

**7.** What idealism could you give up in order to fret less? (For instance: "I need to admit that it's okay to have bland times during marriage.")

## CHAPTER 7
## His Buried Insecurity

**1.** Men don't always look insecure even when they feel insecure. What insecurities does your husband have that hardly anyone knows about? (For instance: "I know he struggles with sexual curiosities and the need to feel loved," or "His anger is really a cover for his fear of not being taken seriously.")

**2.** Does your husband have the need to look more together than he actually feels? How does he try to project this favorable image? (For instance: "He'll laugh and tell jokes in order to keep people from knowing how discouraged he's been feeling.")

**3.** Looking back over the checklist, which three or four items stand out the most?

4. What could you as a spouse do to make it easier for him to reveal hidden insecurities? (For instance: "He doesn't want criticism; he prefers a patient, listening ear.")

5. In the past, how was conditional love communicated to your husband? (For instance: "He'd be crucified by his parents if they knew he drank beer," or "He never felt like he could live up to his older brother's high standards.")

6. Why is self-acceptance sometimes difficult for him? (For instance: "He was trained to like himself only in direct proportion to high achievement or lack of emotional struggles.")

7. A sign of a secure person is the willingness to admit insecurities. In what circumstances would you like to see your husband become more honest about himself? (For instance: "I'd like to see him become less rigid with the kids, admitting that he had many of their same struggles himself," or "He doesn't always have to appear flawless to his coworkers.")

## CHAPTER 8
## Her Self-Image Struggles

1. How might people detect that you are struggling with your self-image? (For instance: "I sometimes slip into depression," or "I'm too eager to be a people-pleaser.")

2. When you feel insecure, how does it affect your communication at home? (For instance: "I become very compliant and say what others want to hear," or "I nag.")

3. As you look back over the checklist, which three or four items apply most?

4. How have you been trained to let your self-image be determined by people or circumstances? (For instance: "My mother emphasized the need to say all the right things in public," or "My peers would make fun of my social awkwardness.")

5. Knowing your Creator deems you to be valuable, how would this help you feel more sure around judgmental people? (For instance: "I'd keep human opinions of me in better perspective.")

6. What superficial qualities could you de-emphasize in your efforts to have a balanced self-image? (For instance: "My choice of clothing need not be so important," or "Who cares if someone sees me without makeup!")

7. You can feel more positive about yourself as you do a better job of planning your emotional reactions. What emotional responses require more logic and planning? (For instance: "I need to get a better handle on the purpose of my anxious feelings," or "I'd like to have a well-devised scheme to know how to be more genuinely loving to my mate.")

## CHAPTER 9
## Five Keys to Successful Relating

1. Harmonious relationships require focus. What distractions will you need to set aside in order to stay abreast of your growth goals? (For instance: "We need to set aside time each week to just talk about us," or "My work needs to be curtailed so the relationship can have room to flourish.")

2. Look back over the checklist. Which three or four items would you like to more successfully integrate into your lifestyle?

3. To make time a frontline priority, what adjustments could you make? (For instance: "Turn off the TV," or "Put the kids to bed at a reasonable time," or "Trim committee memberships.")

4. Being critical is often easier than being accepting. In what areas could you communicate greater acceptance? (For instance: "I could use a softer tone of voice when speaking opinions," or "I could acknowledge that it's okay to have different parenting styles.")

5. Respect does not have to be earned. It can be given. When could you be more openly respectful? (For instance: "When I'm expressing disagreement, I can still refrain from using accusing language," or "I can forgive willingly.")

6. How could a more insightful understanding of your mate cause you to blame less? (For instance: "Knowing why my spouse feels insecure, I can be less harsh in my judgment when he becomes anxious.")

7. What habits could you change to create a more open atmosphere at home? (For instance: "I could talk more about why I feel as I do," or "I could be less prone to give advice, more inclined to listen patiently.")

## CHAPTER 10
### What If He Won't Change?

**1.** When can you know that you need to ease up on your pressure to make your spouse change for the better? (For instance: "When I find myself habitually resentful," or "When our conversations turn into defensive battles.")

**2.** Look back over the twelve-point checklist. Which three or four items would you like to improve most?

**3.** If you chose to think of your emotional growth in singular terms, how would you be different? (For instance: "I'd accuse less," or "I'd give myself permission to spend more time with people he has previously kept me from.")

**4.** Balance in disclosing your pain to others is the mark of healthy relating. What can you do to find that balance? (For instance: "I need to complain less," or "I'd like to find a good friend to confide in.")

**5.** When are you most inclined to run interference for your mate? (For instance: "I give him advice about social skills more often than he likes," or "I feel I should apologize for him when he acts angry.")

6. How can you guard yourself against potential sexual vulnerability outside the marriage? (For instance: "I can be more careful with whom I share my problems," or "I can choose not to watch movies or television that promote immorality.")


7. Are you willing to forgive? What specifically do you need to forgive your spouse for? (For instance: "I need to quit holding grudges regarding his temper outbursts," or "I'll forgive him of the incidences when he didn't get along with my extended family.")

# About the Author

Les Carter, Ph.D., is a nationally known expert in the field of Christian counseling, with more than eighteen years in private practice. He is a psychotherapist with The Minirth Clinic in Richardson, Texas. Dr. Carter earned his B.A. from Baylor University and his M.Ed. from North Texas State University. He is the author or coauthor of more than twelve books, including *The Anger Workbook, Imperative People, Reflecting the Character of Christ,* and *Broken Vows.*

CPSIA information can be obtained at www.ICGtesting.com
Printed in the USA
LVOW041241080712

289195LV00001B/4/A